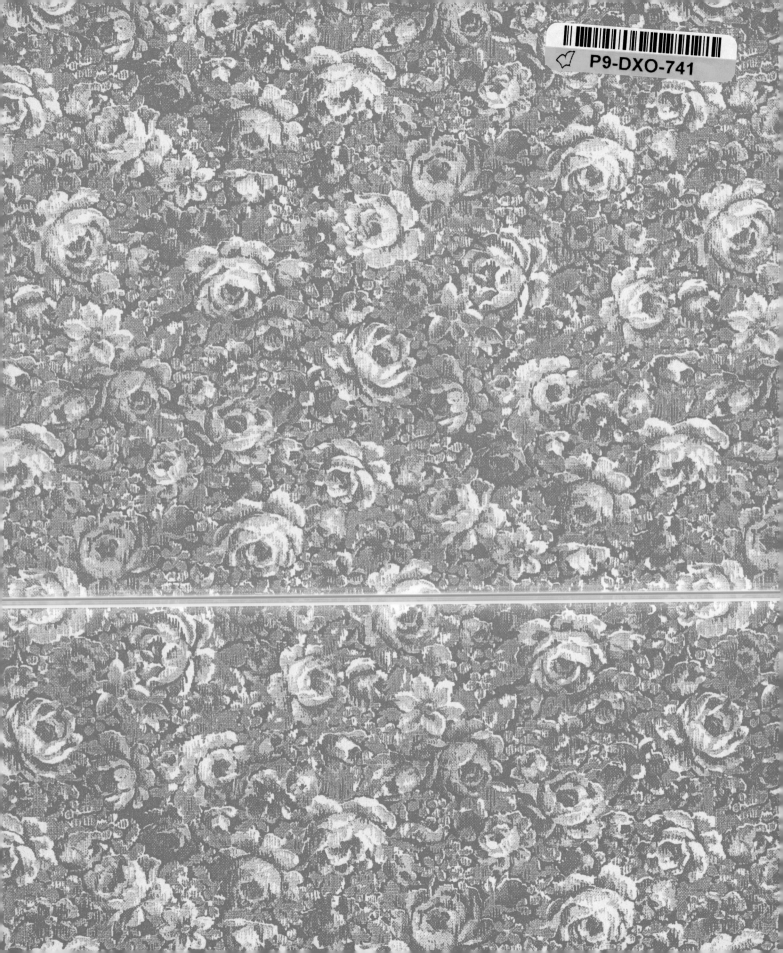
P9-DXO-741

SMALL PATCHWORK & QUILTING

by Leslie Linsley

Photographs by Jon Aron

Illustrations by Robby Savonen

MEREDITH® PRESS

New York, New York

Acknowledgments

Every new book we create involves many talented people. Jon and I are especially grateful to our daughter, Robby Savonen, who spent months working with us to design, create, and write the directions for all the projects. We also want to thank VIP and Peter Pan for enabling us to use their newest lines of fabrics, which are so beautifully designed and easily adaptable to quilt-making.

My mother, Ruth Linsley, Nancy Moore, Suzi Peterson, Karen Schwenk, Kate McCombe, and Robby all contributed their wonderful designs and their sewing and quiltmaking abilities, which have made this book an exciting potpourri of accessible projects. Most of all I want to thank my editor, Maryanne Bannon, who has the rare ability to work with creative people. I appreciate her professionalism as well as her encouragement during the long process of bringing a book to fruition.

All projects are quilted or stuffed with Poly-Fil® from Fairfield Processing Corporation. Wall coverings in the children's rooms are from Wall-Tex and trucks are from Little Tykes.

Meredith® Press is an imprint of Meredith® Books:
President, Book Group: Joseph J. Ward
Vice President, Editorial Director: Elizabeth P. Rice

For Meredith® Press:
Executive Editor: Maryanne Bannon
Associate Editor: Carolyn Mitchell
Copy Editor: Sydne Matus
Proofreader: Carol Anderson
Production Manager: Bill Rose
Book Designer: Remo Cosentino

Copyright © 1993 by Leslie Linsley. All rights reserved. Distributed by Meredith Corporation, Des Moines, Iowa.

Brief quotations may be used in critical articles and reviews. For any other reproduction of the book, however, including electronic, mechanical, photocopying, recording, or other means, written permission must be obtained from the publisher.

ISBN: 0-696-02380-6
Library of Congress Catalog Card Number: 92-085220

Printed in the United States of America
10 9 8 7 6 5 4 3 2 1

Introduction

Anyone who loves patchwork and quilting will enjoy making small projects. While it's satisfying to work on a large project such as a double wedding ring quilt, it's nice to be able to set it aside to make a crib quilt or a wall hanging. And if you're new to the craft of making quilted patchwork, a small quilting project can be very rewarding—it is usually fun to make and you see beautiful results quickly.

Small projects make wonderful gifts. There is such a variety of items from which to choose. Almost any pieced fabric project can be quilted. You might choose to make place mats or Christmas ornaments; duffel, toy, or cosmetic bags; or a pillow, wall hanging, or crib quilt. Imagine welcoming a newborn infant with a handmade quilt. Nothing could be more appreciated. This is the ideal gift because it is practical, pretty, and will be cherished for many years. It even gets better-looking with each washing. Appliqué quilts for Baby can be made with adorable designs. Or you can make patchwork patterns from pastel prints or brightly colored fabrics. It is even possible to complete a crib quilt in a weekend.

Small quilting projects are perfect items to sell at fundraising bazaars. They can be made from scraps of fabric left over from larger projects and are therefore extremely economical. Quilting small projects is an excellent leisure-time activity, especially when pinching pennies and making the most of limited time are important.

My husband, Jon Aron, our newly married daughter, Robby Savonen, her mother-in-law, Nancy Moore, my mother, Ruth Linsley, and I all worked together to design and make most of the projects for this book. We are a family that has been crafting together for a very long time. We especially liked the instant gratification that small projects provided.

Karen Schwenk and Kate McCombe, talented quiltmakers on Nantucket Island, where Jon and I live, generously shared their quilting projects as well. Karen has been quilting for many years and made the Take-Along Quilt on page 103 for her nieces, as well as the Miniature Log Cabin Wall Hanging on page 112. Kate's quilts are sold through The Museum Shop at the Whaling Museum in Nantucket, Massachusetts, and bear the name "Quartermoon Quilts."

Our good friend Suzi Peterson made the Country Barnyard Quilt on page 76. Suzi is the mother of a four-year-old daughter, Lindsay, and is a longtime crafter whose work often appears in our books.

Beyond presenting well-designed projects, our goal was to consider the use of materials and plan the directions with an eye toward economy of both money and time. Sometimes this meant redesigning a project if we felt too much material was required. We often found that the new, less costly design looked better. Our emphasis on economy also meant going over the directions many times to find shortcuts for doing things more efficiently.

We decided that it wouldn't insult anyone's intelligence to have all the step-by-step instructions clearly spelled even though we also included as many cutting and piecing diagrams as needed to make each project as clear as it could be. I learned long ago that even the most beautiful project isn't fun to make if the instructions are difficult to understand.

Each project includes tips when they can help ease the crafting process. Once in a while I discover alternative ways to do things. One way may not be better than another for me, but it might be for you, so I've tried to include this information. When Robby was quilting the Mini Log Cabin Pillows on page 116, for example, she found that narrow strips look better when the quilting stitches are closer to the seam line than we usually recommend.

Because of my readers, each book gets better. You let me know when I've made an error or when you truly like what I've presented, and I appreciate hearing it all, even the criticism. It keeps me on my toes and I learn a lot.

Small Patchwork & Quilting was a rewarding experience from beginning to end. Many of the projects were made while snow flurries drifted over our little island out at sea, and this made the crafting experience quite magical. I hope wherever you live you will enjoy making them as much as we did.

—Leslie Linsley

Dear Quilter:

We know all good things come in small packages. If you've ever received a small quilt as a gift, you've been assured of the truth in that adage. In this latest offering by Meredith Press, Leslie Linsley has created a very special collection of diminutive quilting projects. Quick and uncomplicated, they include coverlets and carry-alls we think you'll love to make and give, and wall hangings and pillows you might be just as happy to keep for yourself.

The sixth volume in our annual quilting series, *Small Patchwork & Quilting* is likely to become your favorite resource for make-in-a-weekend home accents, baby accessories, year-round gifts, and holiday decorations. As with all Meredith Press books, we have tried to bring out the best in crafts by emphasizing the clear instructions, labeled diagrams, full-size templates, and four-color photos involved in making every project a pleasure. In that respect, we hope we've had some *small* measure of success.

Sincerely,

Maryanne Bannon

Executive Editor

4

CONTENTS

QUILTING BASICS

Quilting Terms

The "language" of quilting is used throughout this book to describe the various steps used to make the projects. It is easily learned and will help you to understand the different processes involved in making small quilt projects. When you look at a patchwork or appliquéd project, for example, you'll be knowledgeable about how it was made. This information will also help you to understand directions. They are basic and logical and, if you are new to the craft, will enable you to see how easy it is.

Appliqué
The technique of creating a design by cutting a shape from one fabric and stitching it to a contrasting fabric background.

Backing
The piece of fabric used on the underside of the pieced or appliquéd top of a project. Usually of the same fabric weight, this piece can be made from solid or printed fabric to match the top design. Sometimes the backing is made from the same fabric as that used to create borders on a quilt or wall hanging. I especially like to use an old sheet for the backing on a quilt. The sizes are large enough without adding piecing seams, and an old sheet is nice and soft. When making small projects, one of the fabric pieces from the top can be used for the backing. In this way the project is completely coordinated.

Basting
Securing the top, batting, and backing together with long, loose stitches before quilting. These stitches are removed after each section is quilted.

Batting
The soft lining that makes a quilt puffy and gives it warmth. Batting comes in

various thicknesses, each appropriate for different kinds of projects. Most quilts are made with a thin layer of Poly-Fil®. This thin layer of batting is also used between the top and backing of a pillow that is being quilted. Batting also comes in small, fluffy pieces that are used for stuffing projects such as sachets, pin cushions, and pillows.

Binding

The way the raw edges of fabric are finished. Many quiltmakers cut the backing slightly larger than the top piece so they can bring the extra fabric forward to finish the edges. Contrasting fabric or bias binding is also used. Bias binding can be used for a quick-and-easy way to finish the top edge of a Christmas stocking.

Block

This is often referred to as a square. Geometric or symmetrical pieces of fabric are sewn together to create a design. The finished blocks are then joined to create the finished quilt top. Individual blocks are often large enough to use for a matching pillow. A series of small blocks can be joined to create an interesting pattern for a wall hanging or bench cushion and many other projects.

Borders

Fabric strips that frame the pieced design. A border can be narrow or wide, and sometimes there is more than one border around a quilt, pillow, or wall hanging. Borders often frame quilt blocks and are sometimes made from one of the fabrics or from a contrasting fabric. Borders are often used to extend the size of a quilt top so that it drops down over the sides of the mattress.

Traditionally, quilting patterns are stitched in the borders of a quilt for interest. However, many quilters leave this area free of stitches in order to complete the project in a shorter period of time. When you make small projects, a quilting pattern adds interest to the patchwork top.

Patchwork

Sewing together of fabric pieces to create an entire design. Sometimes the shapes form a geometric block. The blocks are then sewn together to make up the completed project.

Piecing

Joining patchwork pieces together to form a design on the block.

Quilting

Stitching together two layers of fabric with a layer of batting in between.

Quilting Patterns

The lines or markings on the fabric that make up the design. Small hand or machine stitches quilt along these lines, which might be straight or curved or made up of elaborate, curlicued patterns. Small quilting stitches can also follow the seam lines where pieces of fabric are joined. Or a quilting pattern can be created by stitching a grid or diamonds over the entire fabric.

Sashes or Strips

The narrow pieces of fabric used to frame the individual blocks and join them together. They are often created in a contrasting color.

Setting

Joining the quilt blocks to form the finished top piece of a quilt.

Template

A pattern that is rigid and full-size. It can be cut from cardboard or plastic and is used to trace the design elements. Some quilters use sandpaper for their templates because they are of the acceptable weight and won't slide on the fabric. When cutting the fabric, you will usually add ¼ inch for a seam allowance. When the pattern piece for any project in this book calls for a template, it will state whether a seam allowance is included.

Top

The top of a quilting project is the front layer of fabric with the right side showing. Patchwork or appliqué pieces create the top fabric.

Materials for Quilting

Cutting Board

This is a handy item for the quick measuring and cutting methods you'll use to make quilting projects. It is available in fabric stores or from mail-order sources.

Cutting Wheel

A cutting wheel (rotary cutter) is useful for cutting strips of fabric for strip-piecing. Place a metal straightedge on the fabric and run the circular blade of the cutting wheel along the side of the straightedge.

Fabric

You can never have too many different fabric patterns when designing a quilting project. Fabric is the main concern: what kind, how much to buy, and what colors or prints will work together.

Almost every type of fabric has been used to make quilts and quilting projects. However, most quilters prefer cotton and, if necessary, will settle for a cotton/polyester blend in order to find the right color or pattern for the project. Pure cotton should be washed before it is used. This removes any sizing in the fabric and allows for shrinkage.

When collecting a variety of fabric prints for your quilting projects, it's a good idea to have a selection of lights and darks. The colors and patterns of the fabric will greatly affect the design. Calico has always been used for quilting projects. The small, overall prints can be used effectively together and there is a wide variety of colors to choose from.

Iron

Have you ever known anyone to sew without an iron next to the sewing machine? It's impossible to do without it. If you are doing patchwork, it's handy to pad a stool or chair with a piece of batting and place the iron next to you by the sewing machine. As you piece the fabric, you can iron the seams without getting up. Use a steam setting.

Markers

Sometimes a pattern or design has to be traced from the book and transferred to the fabric. When you want an overall quilting design, you'll need lines to follow. A soft pencil is good for these purposes. Some quilters use a water-soluble pen to mark quilting lines on their fabric and then remove them with a mister after stitching.

Needles

All of the projects in this book are stitched on a sewing machine. The quilting can be done by hand or on the machine. If you are stitching by hand, you should buy #7 and #8 sharps, which are the most common sizes for hand-quilting. They are often called "betweens."

Ruler and Yardstick

These are essential. A metal ruler can be used as a straightedge for the most accurate cutting. Use the yardstick for cutting lengths of fabric where you must mark and cut at least 36 inches at one time.

The width of the yardstick is often used to mark a grid pattern for quilting. You simply draw the first line, then flip the yardstick over and continue to mark lines without removing the yardstick from the fabric. You will have a perfect 1-inch grid.

Scissors

Good-quality scissors are essential for accurately cutting your fabric. Do not use your fabric scissors to cut paper. This will ruin your scissors.

Templates

Shirt cardboard or manila oak tag used for filing folders is ideal for cutting templates. Acetate is also a good material because you'll get clean, crisp edges and you can see through it. Templates will be used for appliqué pieces when a repeat design is required. If you are cutting one design, you can simply pin the paper pattern to the fabric as a cutting guide.

Thimble

When quilting, you will be taking 3 to 6 stitches at a time through 3 layers of fabric. It takes a while to get used to using a thimble, but most quilters find that it makes this task painless and more fun.

Thread

Match the thread to the color of the fabric. Cotton-blend thread is best for appliqué and piecing.

Quilting Techniques

Appliqué

To *hand-appliqué*, cut out each pattern piece using a template. If there is no seam allowance on your template, add ¼ to ⅜ inch all around when cutting. Stay-stitch along seam allowance (see Figure 1). Place the template on the back of the fabric and press all edges over the template edges. If the appliqué is curved, clip all edges to the seam line before turning (see Figure 2).

Remove template and pin the appliqué in place on the background fabric and blindstitch or whipstitch it all around. The appliquéd fabric is then backed with batting before you quilt around the design. When you quilt, use short running stitches around the inside edge of the appliqué.

To *machine-appliqué*, cut the fabric without a seam allowance. Edges need not be turned. Pin the appliqué in position on the fabric and zigzag-stitch around the edges.

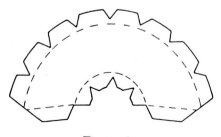

Figure 1   Figure 2

Cutting

Before cutting out each pattern piece, especially when long strips and borders are called for, carefully plan the layout of the pieces on your fabric. You do not want to begin by cutting the smallest pieces and end up without enough fabric for the larger pieces.

Enlarging a Design

If you'd like to enlarge the size of a quilt or wall hanging, there are several approaches, but the most important thing to remember is to buy enough extra fabric to accommodate the increased size.

If the project is made up of a series of connecting blocks, simply add more quilt blocks to each row in either direction. Or you can add a border around the outside. If a border is part of the original design, make it wider or add another border in another fabric to go with the project.

If you want to enlarge or decrease the size of a pattern piece or design, you can do so on a copying machine. While all the templates in this book are full-size, if a pattern, such as one for a Christmas stocking, is too large for the page, it will be shown on a grid. Each square on the grid equals 1 inch. This means that you will transfer or copy the design onto graph paper marked with 1-inch squares. Begin by counting the number of squares on the pattern in the book. Number them horizontally and again vertically. Count the same number of squares on your larger graph and number them in the same way. Copy the design onto your grid one square at a time.

Estimating Amount of Fabric

The fabric used for all of the projects is 45 inches wide. All measurements are figured with a 1/4-inch seam allowance.

If a quilt size for any project shown here isn't the right size for your bed, it can be changed by adding to or subtracting from the border measurements. This shouldn't change the basic design.

The amount of fabric needed for all projects in the book has been figured out and listed at the beginning of each project. It's always a good idea to buy a little extra to allow for any cutting or stitching errors.

Hem Stitch

This is often used to finish the edges of an appliqué. Use thread to match the fabric. Bring the needle up from the wrong side of the fabric through the folded edge of the appliqué. Insert the needle on the diagonal into the top of the fabric close to the appliqué and slightly ahead of the first stitch.

Making a Template

Trace the designs or patterns on tracing paper using a pencil and straightedge. It's important to do this accurately. Mark each piece with an identifying mark or number and note the number of pieces to be cut from this pattern piece. You can use the pattern piece by pinning it to the corresponding fabric and cutting or you can mount it to cardboard with spray adhesive. Apply the glue to the back of the pattern piece, place it firmly on a piece of cardboard or oak tag slightly larger than the pattern piece, and smooth down with your hand. Cut around the pattern to make your template. You can also make a template from clear acetate. Place a piece of acetate over the pattern and trace around the design with a pen as you would on tracing paper. Cut out the exact shape, which includes a ¼-inch seam allowance.

Determine which fabric will be used for each template. Consider the grain of the fabric and the direction of the print when placing your templates. Lay the template on the fabric, hold firmly in position, and draw around the outline with a pencil or fabric marker. Mark the back of each piece with the correct number as indicated in the piecing directions. It's a good idea to save templates in an envelope marked with the name of the project.

Piecing the Backing

You may have to piece panels together for the back of a quilt, tablecloth, or wall hanging in order to get the correct size. Use the full width of fabric, usually 45 inches, cut to the appropriate length. Cut another piece the same size. Then cut the second strip of fabric in half lengthwise so that you have two narrow strips of the same size. Join these two matching panels to each long-sided edge of the large, center panel to avoid having a seam down the middle of the quilt backing. Press seams open.

Sewing Curves

Before turning a curved appliqué piece, stay-stitch along the seam line, then clip or notch evenly spaced cuts along the edge in the seam allowance. Clip all inward curves and notch all outward curves. When the fabric is turned under, it will lie flat.

Sewing Inside Corner Edge

Place a pin across the point of the stitches and clip up to the stitches in the seam allowance in order to turn the fabric under.

Sewing Outside Corner Edge

Once you've stitched around a corner, clip off half the seam allowance across the point. Turn fabric back, press seams open, and trim excess fabric.

Sewing Points

Many traditional quilt patterns are created from triangles, diamonds, and similar shapes. The points present a challenge and require special care.

When stitching 2 such pieces together, sew along the stitch line, but do not sew into the seam allowance at each point (see Figure 3). It helps to mark the finished points with a pin so that you can begin and end your seams at these marks.

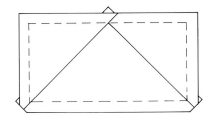

Figure 3

Transferring a Design

Trace the pattern pieces or quilting design from the book. Place a piece of dressmaker's tracing (carbon) paper on the right side of the fabric with the carbon side down and tracing paper on top. Go over all pattern lines with a tracing wheel or ballpoint pen to transfer the design. Remove the carbon and tracing.

Turning Corners

It's often a bit difficult to turn corners and continue a seam line. Figure 4 shows the 3 pieces to be joined. With right sides facing, stitch piece A to piece B as shown in Figure 5. Next, join C to A as shown in Figure 6. Leave the needle down in the fabric. Lift the presser foot and clip the seam to the needle. Slide B under C and adjust so the edges of B align with C. Lower the presser foot and stitch along the seam line (see Figure 7).

Figure 4

Figure 5

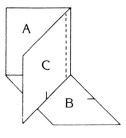

Figure 6

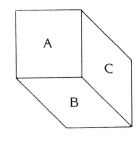

Figure 7

13

How to Quilt

Quilting is the means by which you sew layers of fabric and batting together to produce a padded fabric held together by stitching. The quilting process, generally the finishing step in appliqué and patchwork projects, is what makes a project interesting and gives it a textured look.

Basting

Before quilting, you will baste the quilt top, batting, and backing together. To avoid a lump of filler at any point, begin at the center of the top and baste outward with long, loose stitches to create a sunburst pattern. There should be about 6 inches between the basted lines at the edges of the quilt. Baste from the top only. These stitches will be cut away as you do your quilting.

Hand-Quilting

Thread your needle and knot one end as for regular hand-sewing. Bring the needle up through the back to the front and give the knotted end a good tug to pull it through the backing fabric into the batting. Keep your thread fairly short (about 18 inches) and take small running stitches. Follow your pre-marked quilting pattern.

Machine-Quilting

This quicker way to create a quilted look does not have the same rich look of authentic, early quilting that hand-stitching has. It is best to machine-quilt only when the batting isn't too thick. Although the piecing of these quilts can be finished in a weekend, I still recommend hand-quilting in a leisurely fashion unless it's more important that the project be completed quickly.

When machine-quilting, set the thread tension at approximately 6 stitches to the inch so that the stitching looks like hand-stitching. Taking this precaution will assure that the absence of hand-stitching does not detract from the design (see Figure 8).

Overall Quilting

When you want to fill large areas of the background with quilting, choose a simple design. The background quilting should not interfere with the patchwork or appliqué elements.

To ensure accurate spacing, make grid patterns of squares or diamond shapes with a yardstick or masking tape. For a quick-and-easy method, lay a yardstick diagonally across the fabric and mark the material lightly with a

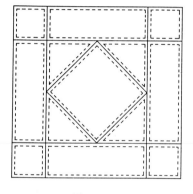

Figure 8

Figure 9

pencil. Without removing the yardstick, turn it over and mark along the edge once again. Continue across the fabric to the opposite edge. You will have perfect 1-inch spaces between each line. Lay the yardstick across the fabric at the corner opposite where you began and repeat the process to create a 1-inch grid across the top of the fabric (see Figure 9). Stitch along these lines. The stitching will hide the pencil lines.

Quick-and-Easy Methods

Assembly-Line Piecing

When a project calls for a series of the same types of pieces, it's easy to feed them through the machine one right after another rather than one at a time. After you've stitched the first set of pieces together, leave the presser foot down and run the machine for a few stitches beyond the end of the fabric. Then, feed the next set of fabric pieces through the machine and continue stitching. You can repeat this as many times as needed. When you have a string of the desired number of assembled pieces, clip the threads between and press all seams to one side.

Pressing Seams

Quilters are divided on the issue of whether to press seams open or to one side. Many believe that a quilt is stronger if seams are pressed to one side. However, if you are making a wall hanging or a quilt that will not get much wear and tear, the pieced top will look neater if the seams are pressed open. If the piecing has been done on a machine, it will have enough strength to withstand repeated washings no matter how the seams are pressed. If you are using light and dark fabrics stitched together, it is always best to press the seams to the dark side so the fabric doesn't show through. The important thing is to press the seams each time you stitch fabric pieces together.

Strip-Piecing

This is the method by which you sew strips of different fabrics together and then cut them into units that are arranged to make up the entire quilt top. Rather than cutting and sewing individual squares together over and over again, 2 or more strips of fabric are sewn together and then cut into segments that are of the same dimensions. These units are then arranged and stitched together in different positions to form the quilt pattern.

Finishing Touches for Pillows

Adding a Ruffle

A ruffle can be added to a pillow top with or without piping. For a 4-inch-wide ruffle, you will cut a strip 8½ inches wide and 2 times the perimeter of the pillow. You might have to join strips to make one continuous length of fabric. With right sides facing and raw edges aligned, sew the strips together end to end to make one continuous loop. Fold the strip in half lengthwise with wrong sides facing and press.

Divide the ruffle into 4 sections and mark with pins. These marks represent the corners on your pillow. Next, mark the center of each side, halfway between 2 corner pins. With the raw edges of the ruffle strip aligned with the raw edges of the outside top of the pillow, gather and pin the ruffle evenly all around with a bit of extra fullness at each corner. Stitch around ¼ inch from the outside edge. Remove pins.

With right sides facing, pin the backing fabric to the pillow top with the ruffle in between. Using the ruffle stitches as a guide, stitch around 3 sides and 4 corners. Remove pins and clip excess fabric around seam allowance and corners. Turn right side out and pull ruffle to outside.

Adding Piping

Contrasting or matching piping is a nice way to finish the edges of a pillow or seat cushion. The project has a crisp and professional look when it is trimmed with matching fabric-covered piping. The piping can be very narrow, as for a small sachet, or quite fat if used on an oversized throw pillow. The cording for piping is sold by the yard in most fabric shops and is quite inexpensive. It looks like soft rope.

Measure around the pillow edge and add an extra inch. Cut lengths of bias fabric 1½ inches wide and stitch them together to create a strip long enough to go around the pillow, plus an extra inch.

Turn the short raw edges of the fabric strip under ¼ inch and press. Cut the cording strip 1 inch shorter than the strip of fabric and place it in the center of the strip. Fold the fabric over the cording so the long raw edges are aligned with the cord encased inside.

Using the zipper foot on your sewing machine, stitch along the fabric as close to the cording as possible. Do not stitch the last ½ inch of the fabric together. The cording will not reach the end of the fabric.

Begin at the center of one edge of the pillow top and pin piping all around with raw edges aligned. Where the 2 ends meet, overlap the extra fabric so that the cording comes together inside the fabric channel. Stitch around.

With right sides facing and raw edges aligned, pin the backing fabric piece to the top with the piping in between. Stitch around 3 sides and 4 corners, leaving a few inches open on one side for turning. Trim the seam allowance and clip off the corners. Turn right side out and finish the pillow as directed in each project.

Slip Stitch

Once a pillow is stuffed with Poly-Fil® or a pillow form, the easiest way to close the open side is with the slip stitch. Fold under the seam allowance on one side of the opening and pin the folded edge over the raw edges of the opposite side of the fabric.

Insert the needle through the bottom layer of the fabric right at the seam line at one end of the opening. Take a small stitch through the fold on the top layer, then through the seam line on the bottom layer. Continue in this way so that the seam line matches the area that has been machine-stitched from the wrong side.

Zipper

For easy removal of a pillow cover, a zipper can be stitched to the open side rather than being closed with a slip stitch. The directions for inserting a zipper are on the package. Buy a zipper 2 inches shorter than the length of the finished pillow in a color to match your fabric.

Welcome Banner

A welcome banner makes an interesting decoration in a hallway or over a fireplace. This project would make a lovely housewarming gift as well. The traditional country theme is expressed in cranberry and green colors combined with a house design. The finished size is 13×20 inches.

Materials

Note: All yardages are figured for 45-inch-wide fabric.

    ½ yard green solid (includes backing)
    ¼ yard white or bleached muslin solid
    ¼ yard cranberry calico
    small piece of cranberry solid
    scraps of red, blue, and green calicos
    quilt batting 14×21 inches
    tracing paper
    cardboard
    Velcro® tabs for hanging

Cutting List

Note: All measurements include a ¼-inch seam allowance.

Trace patterns A, B, C, D, E, F, G, Y, and Z and transfer to cardboard for templates (see page 11).

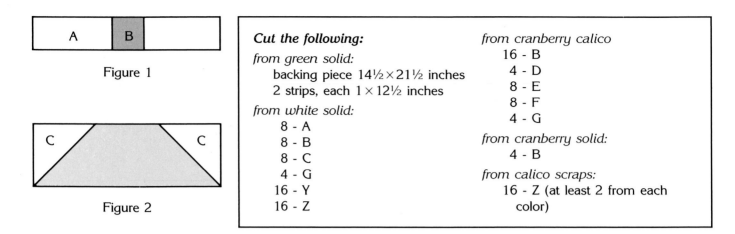

Figure 1

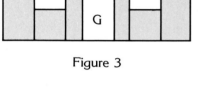

Figure 2

Cut the following:

from green solid:
    backing piece 14½ × 21½ inches
    2 strips, each 1 × 12½ inches

from white solid:
    8 - A
    8 - B
    8 - C
    4 - G
    16 - Y
    16 - Z

from cranberry calico
    16 - B
    4 - D
    8 - E
    8 - F
    4 - G

from cranberry solid:
    4 - B

from calico scraps:
    16 - Z (at least 2 from each
       color)

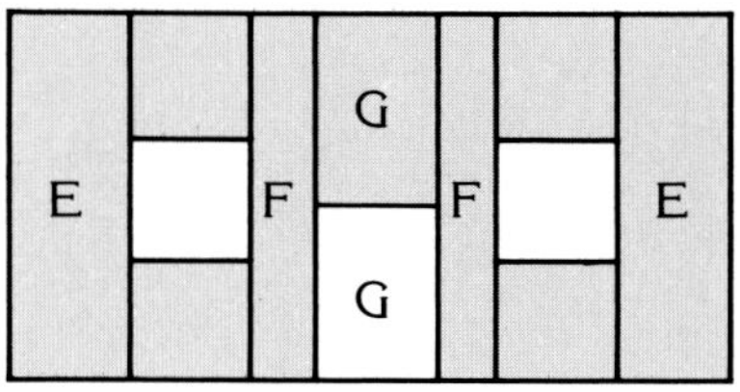

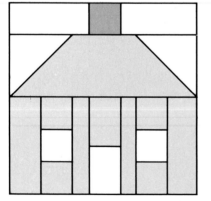

Figure 3

Directions

To make a house block

1. With right sides facing, stitch the short edge of a white A piece to a cranberry solid B piece.

2. Next, stitch this to the short edge of another white piece (Figure 1).

3. With right sides facing, stitch the diagonal edge of a white C piece to each slanted side of a cranberry calico D piece (Figure 2). Press seams to the dark side. These are your 2 top sections.

4. With right sides facing, stitch a cranberry calico B piece to a white B piece, followed by another calico B piece to make a vertical strip. Press seams to one side. Make 2 strips in this way.

5. Stitch a cranberry calico G piece to a white G piece to make a vertical strip. Press seams to one side.

6. With right sides facing, stitch the long edge of an E piece to the long edge of the B strip made in step 4. Press seams to one side.

7. Continue by joining a cranberry calico F piece to the other edge of the B strip, followed by the G strip made in step 5. Stitch this to another F piece, then to the other B strip, followed by an E piece (Figure 3). This is the bottom section of the block. Press seams to one side.

8. With right sides facing, stitch the top 2 sections together along the long edge. Next, stitch the bottom long edge of the top section to the top edge of the bottom section to make a block (Figure 4). Press seams to one side. Make 4 blocks in this way.

To make border blocks

1. With right sides facing, stitch a white Z piece to a calico Z piece along the diagonal to make a square (Figure 5). Press seams to one side. Make 2 squares in this way.

2. Next, stitch each pieced square to a white Y piece to make a rectangle.

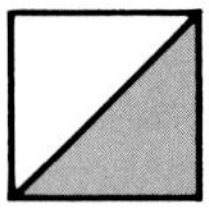

Figure 4

Figure 5

3. With right sides facing and seams aligned, stitch the 2 rectangles together so that the white squares are in opposite corners to make a block (Figure 6). Press seams to one side. Make 8 blocks in this way, using the same color for the 2 triangles in each block.

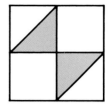

Figure 6

To assemble banner

Refer to the assembly diagram.

1. With right sides facing, stitch the right side of a house block to the left side of another house block to make a row. Repeat with the 2 other house blocks. Press seams to one side.

2. With right sides facing and seams aligned, stitch the bottom edge of one row to the top edge of the other row. Press seams to one side.

3. With right sides facing, attach a $1 \times 12\frac{1}{2}$-inch green strip to each side of the quilt top.

4. With right sides facing, stitch 4 triangle blocks together in a vertical row. Make 2 vertical rows. Press seams to one side.

5. Next, attach a vertical row to each side of the banner. Press seams to one side.

To quilt

1. With right sides facing and batting between, pin the top and the backing together.

2. Baste all 3 layers together with long, loose stitches in a sunburst pattern (see page 14).

3. Using small running stitches, quilt $\frac{1}{4}$ inch on each side of the seam lines, stopping $\frac{1}{2}$ inch in from each raw edge around the outside.

To finish

1. When all quilting has been completed, remove basting stitches.

2. Trim batting $\frac{1}{4}$ inch smaller than the banner top all around.

3. Turn the raw edges of the backing to the inside $\frac{1}{4}$ inch on each side and press.

4. Fold the backing over onto the banner top so there is a $\frac{1}{2}$-inch green border all around. Whipstitch to the top.

To hang

Attach Velcro® tabs to the back of each top corner and in the center. Attach corresponding tabs to the wall where the banner will hang.

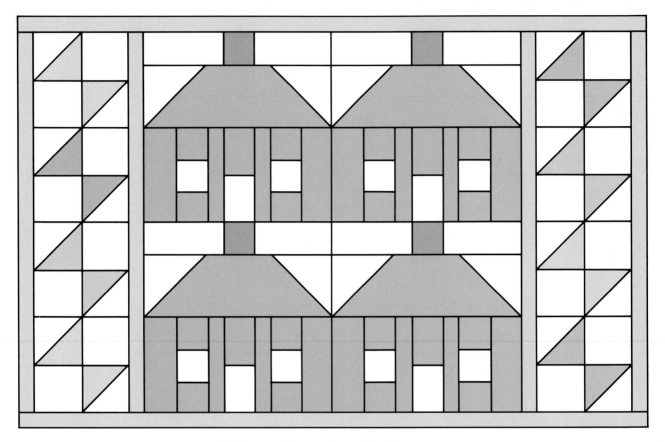

Welcome Banner Assembly Diagram

WELCOME BANNER TEMPLATES

A

C

E

F

B

D

G

Y

Z

23

Country Pillows

The pattern is the same for all three of these cheerful pillows. The colors are rearranged to make each look different. The finished size is 16 × 16 inches.

Materials (for 3 pillows)

Note: All yardages are figured for 45-inch-wide fabric.

2 yards cording for each pillow
½ yard cranberry print (includes 1 backing)
½ yard navy blue print
½ yard white print (includes 1 backing)
½ yard hunter green print (includes 1 backing)
thin quilt batting
stuffing or 16-inch pillow forms
tracing paper and thin cardboard
14-inch zipper for each pillow (optional)

Cutting List

Note: All measurements and templates include a ¼-inch seam allowance.

Trace patterns A, B, and C and transfer to cardboard for templates (see page 11). On the wrong side of each fabric, trace around the specified template.

For Pillow 1 cut the following:

from cranberry print:
   4 - A
   4 - B

from navy blue print:
   8 - B
   1 - C

from white print:
   4 - A

from hunter green print:
   4 - B
   backing piece 17 × 17 inches

For Pillow 2 cut the following:

from cranberry print:
   4 - B

from navy blue print:
   4 - A
   8 - B

from white print:
   1 - C
   backing piece 17 × 17 inches

from hunter green print:
   4 - A
   4 - B

For Pillow 3 cut the following:

from cranberry print:
   4 - B
   1 - C
   backing piece 17 × 17 inches

from navy blue print:
   4 - A
   4 - B

from white print:
   4 - A

from hunter green print:
   8 - B

Directions

Figure 1

Figure 2

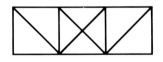

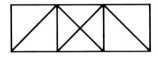

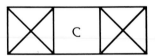

Figure 3

Pillow 1

Refer to the assembly diagram for Pillow 1.

1. With right sides facing, stitch a cranberry A to a white A to make a square as shown in Figure 1. Open seams and press. Make 4.

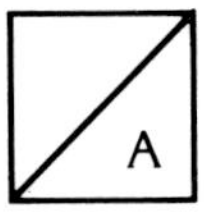

2. With right sides facing, stitch a blue B to a red B along one short edge to make a larger triangle. Next, stitch a blue B to a green B in the same way. Open seams and press.

3. With right sides facing, stitch the 2 pieced triangles together to make a square as shown in Figure 2. Make 4.

To make pillow top

Refer to Figure 3.

1. With right sides facing, stitch 3 squares together to make a row. Make 3 rows according to Figure 3. Open seams and press.

2. Next, stitch the 3 rows together. Open seams and press.

To quilt

1. Cut a piece of batting 17 × 17 inches and pin to the back of the patchwork pillow top.

2. Using small running stitches, quilt ¼ inch on each side of all seam lines.

3. When quilting is completed, remove the pins and trim the batting to the same size as the pillow top.

To finish

You can either use premade piping for the pillow trim or make your own to match the fabric. You will have to stitch short pieces together to create one long strip of fabric to cover the cording. Or, you can buy a package of bias binding in a color to match one of the fabrics.

1. See page 16 for making and attaching piping to the pillow top.

2. With right sides facing, pin the pillow top to the green backing piece with the piping between.

3. Using the piping stitches as a guide, stitch around 3 sides and 4 corners.

4. Clip the corners and turn right side out.

5. Stuff the pillow to desired firmness. Turn the raw edges of the opening to the inside and slip-stitch closed or insert a zipper according to package directions (see page 17).

Pillow 2

Refer to the assembly diagram for Pillow 2. Using the fabric colors shown there, follow directions for Pillow 1. The backing is white and the piping is made from the white print to match.

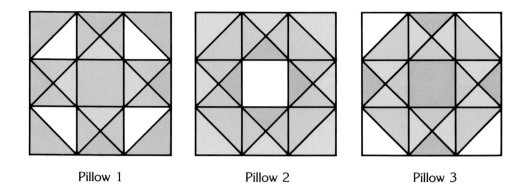

Pillow 1   Pillow 2   Pillow 3

Pillow 3

Refer to the assembly diagram for Pillow 3. Using the fabric colors shown there, follow directions for Pillow 1. The backing is cranberry and the piping is made from the cranberry print.

COUNTRY PILLOWS TEMPLATES

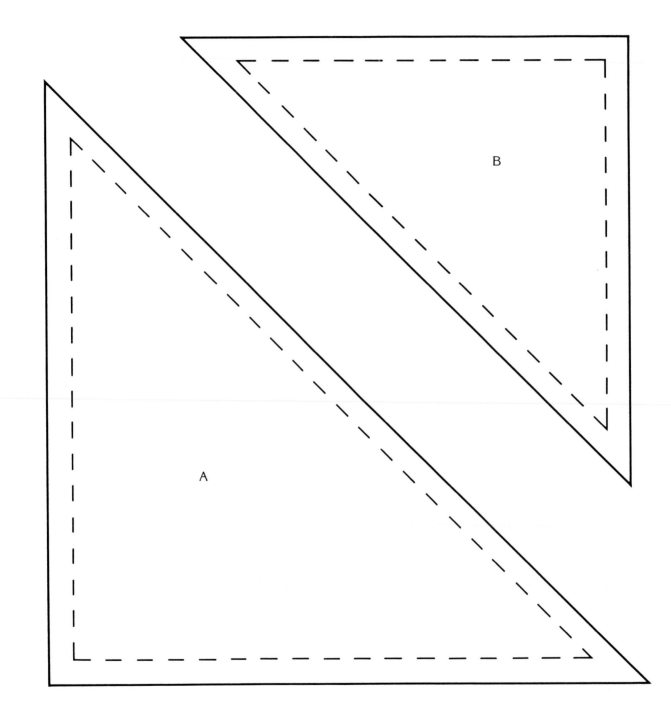

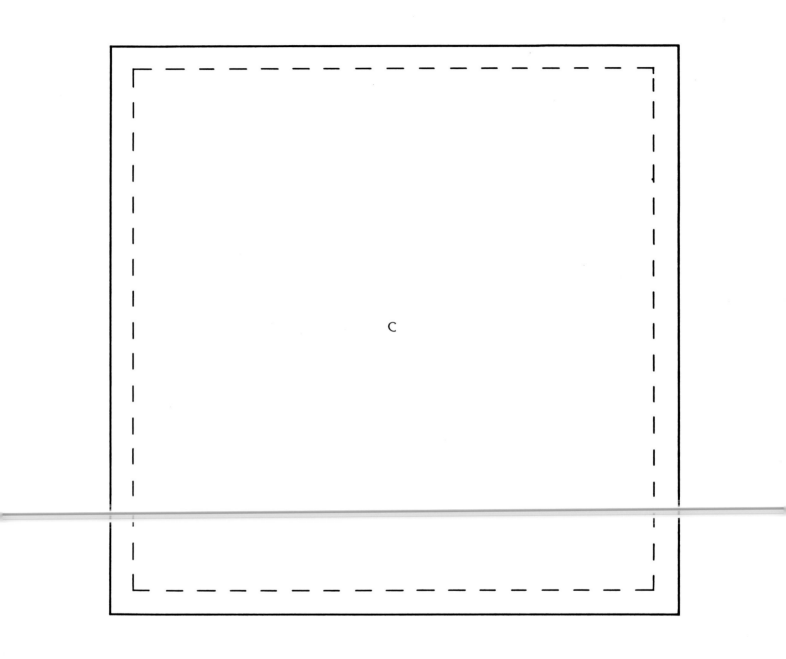

C

Pretty Place Mats

Pretty place mats and matching napkins can be expensive to buy, yet they cost so little to make. And it's so easy to make a set to match the fabrics in your house or to personalize them for gift giving by using favorite colors and prints. It's a great way to use scraps. The finished mat is 12½ × 16½ inches.

Materials (for 2 place mats)

Note: All yardages are figured for 45-inch-wide fabric.

   1 yard calico (includes backing)
   ½ yard calico 2
   ½ yard calico 3
   ½ yard thin quilt batting
   tracing paper
   cardboard

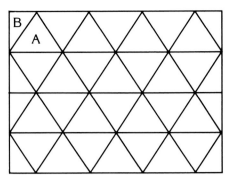

Figure 1

Cutting List

Note: All templates and measurements include a ½-inch seam allowance.

Trace patterns A and B and transfer to cardboard for templates (see page 11). Mark the top and bottom of Template A since the bottom edge is longer than the sides.

Cut the following:	from calicos 1, 2, and 3 (try to evenly distribute pieces to be cut):

from calico 1:
   2 backing pieces, each
      13½ × 17½ inches
	56 - A
	16 - B (8 of them in reverse)

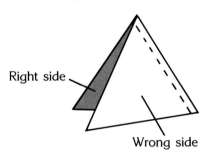

Figure 2

Directions

Each place mat uses 28 A pieces and 8 B pieces (4 in reverse). Arrange your pieces in 4 rows, alternating the different calico prints according to the layout in Figure 1.

1. With right sides facing, stitch 2 A pieces together along one side edge as shown in Figure 2. Press seams to one side.

2. Continue to stitch all 7 A pieces together in this way to make a row.

3. Refer to your layout and, with right sides facing, stitch a B piece to each end of the row. Press seams to one side.

4. Make all 4 rows this way, following the layout in Figure 1.

5. With right sides facing, stitch the bottom edge of the first row to the top edge of the second row, taking care to match the points of the triangles. Press seams to one side.

6. Continue to join all 4 rows in this way.

To finish

1. Cut the batting piece ¼ inch smaller than the place mat top all around.

2. With wrong sides facing, pin top, batting, and backing together.

3. Tack the 3 layers together with 1 or 2 tiny stitches at each triangle point.

4. Fold the raw edges of the backing forward ¼ inch on each side and press.

Next, fold each side of the backing over again onto the top of the place mat to create a ¼-inch border all around the top. Press and pin.

5. Machine- or slip-stitch all around.

Napkins

Cut 18-inch squares from any of the prints and hem all around for matching napkins. You can make 4 napkins from a yard of fabric.

PRETTY PLACE MATS TEMPLATES

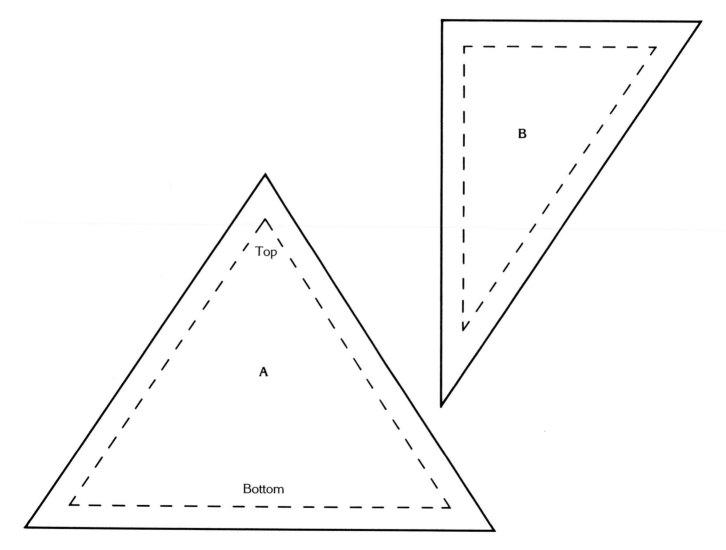

Fence Rail Seat Cushion

You can adapt most traditional quilt patterns to make a custom cushion to fit a bench, window seat, or blanket chest. The fence rail pattern is one that can easily be adapted to fit seats of different sizes. For our cushion we used 6-inch squares, with 2 rows of 5 squares each. We then added borders around each edge to create the size needed. Our finished cushion is 14 × 32 inches. It is 2 inches thick, so there is a 2-inch boxing strip all around.

Materials

Note: All yardages are figured for 45-inch-wide fabric.

    1 yard blue calico (backing, boxing strip, piping)
    ¼ yard each of 6 different blue calicos ranging from dark to light
    cording to go around entire seat
    20-inch white zipper
    1 piece of foam 2 inches thick to fit cushion

Cutting List

Note: All measurements include a ¼-inch seam allowance.

Cut the following:

from 1-yard blue calico:
    backing piece, 14½ × 32½ inches, or to fit your cushion
    2 border pieces, each 1½ × 12½ inches, or to fit your cushion
    2 border pieces, each 1 × 32½ inches, or to fit your cushion
    2 boxing strips for zipper, each 1½ × 20½ inches, or to fit your cushion

    2 boxing strips, each 2½ × 19½ inches, or to fit your cushion
    1 boxing strip, 2½ × 32½ inches, or to fit your cushion

from each of six ¼-yard blue calicos:
    1½-inch-wide-strips

Directions

Use the strip-piecing method (page 16) for this project.

1. Going from dark to light, arrange 6 strips in a row.

2. With right sides facing, stitch the first 2 strips together along one long edge. Press seams to one side.

3. Continue to join all 6 strips in this way. Press seams to one side.

4. Measure and mark across the pieced strips in 6½-inch segments (see Figure 1). Cut as many blocks as you will need for your cushion. We used 10.

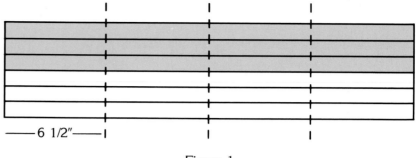

Figure 1

Note: For 4-inch blocks use 4 strips and cut 4½-inch segments. For 5-inch blocks use 5 strips and cut 5½-inch segments. You can add borders to make up any size difference.

To assemble top

1. With right sides facing, stitch 2 blocks together, one with the strips in a vertical direction and one with the strips in a horizontal direction (see Figure 2). Press seams to one side.

2. Continue to join blocks in this way to make a row of 5 blocks.

3. For the second row, start with a block of strips in a horizontal direction (see Figure 3).

4. With right sides facing, stitch the 2 rows together as shown in Figure 3. Press seams to one side.

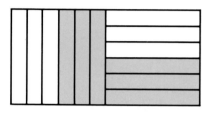

Figure 2

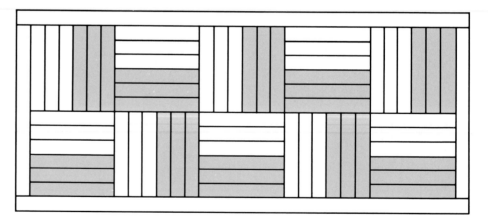

Figure 3

To add borders

Note: Our borders are made of strips 1½ × 12½ inches for the sides and 1 × 32½ inches for the top and bottom.

1. With right sides facing, join the shorter strips to each side of the pieced top. Press seams to one side.

34

2. With right sides facing, join the longer strips to the top and bottom edges of the pieced top in the same way. Press seams.

To make piping

1. To make piping, use one of the blue calicos and refer to page 16.

2. With raw edges aligned, pin the piping to the right side of the pieced top. Clip into the seam allowance at each corner so the piping will turn neatly.

3. Using the piping stitches as a guide, stitch all around.

To make boxing strip

1. Cut 2 strips, each $1\frac{1}{2} \times 20\frac{1}{2}$ inches (or dimensions for your cushion). With right sides facing, attach the zipper (see package for directions).
2. Cut 2 strips, each $2\frac{1}{2} \times 19\frac{1}{2}$ inches (or dimensions for your cushion) for the side bands, which come around to meet the zipper piece.
3. Next, cut a strip $2\frac{1}{2} \times 32\frac{1}{2}$ inches (or dimensions for your cushion) for the front band.
4. With right sides facing, stitch each side band to the short ends of the front band to make a long strip.
5. Next, fold each raw end under $\frac{1}{4}$ inch and stitch.

To assemble seat cushion

1. With right sides facing, pin the top edge of the long band piece to the pieced top. Stitch across the front edge, matching the seams at the corners. Continue to stitch down each side, bringing the ends around to the back, as shown in Figure 4.
2. Pin the zipper piece across the back, overlapping the raw edges over the finished ends of the other piece (see Figure 4). The piping will be between the band and the pieced top.
3. Using the piping stitches as a guide, stitch all around.
4. With right sides facing, pin the bottom edge of the band piece to the backing piece. Stitch all around.
5. Open the zipper and turn cushion cover right side out.
6. Cut a piece of 2-inch foam to the finished cushion size and insert. Close zipper.

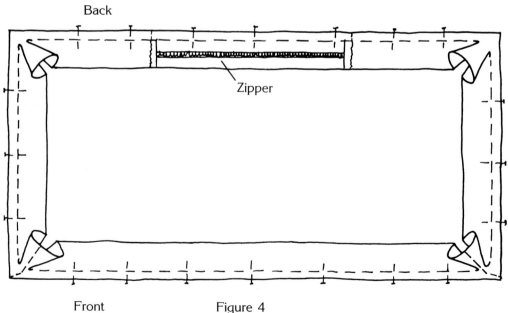

Back

Zipper

Front   Figure 4

Windowpane Wall Hanging

This small square wall hanging was designed by Nancy Moore. She chose different shades of blue to create a nighttime window scene, then used silver thread and sequins to add stars and a moon for celestial sparkle. The finished size is 21 × 21 inches.

Materials

Note: All yardages are figured for 45-inch-wide fabric.

    1 yard medium turquoise print (includes backing)
    ¼ yard dark turquoise
    ¼ yard light turquoise
    thin quilt batting 23 × 23 inches
    turquoise thread for quilting
    silver thread
    silver stars and moon sequins (available in crafts and fabric stores)
    tracing paper
    cardboard
    Velcro® tabs for hanging

Cutting List

Note: All measurements include a ¼-inch seam allowance.

Trace patterns A and B and transfer to cardboard for templates (see page 11). Trace around the templates on the fabrics indicated below.

Cut the following:	20 - B
from dark turquoise solid:	*from light turquoise solid:*
20 - A	20 - B (in reverse)
from medium turquoise print:	
backing piece, 22½ × 22½ inches	

Directions

To make a block

1. With right sides facing, stitch the side edge of an A piece to the matching side edge of a print B piece, stopping ¼ inch from the bottom edge of the A piece as shown in Figure 1. Press seams to one side (see Figure 2).

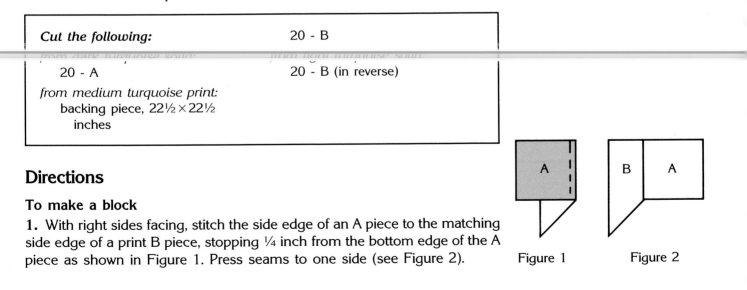

Figure 1   Figure 2

2. Next, stitch a light turquoise B piece to the bottom edge of the A piece as shown in Figure 3. When you get to the inside corner, match the 2 angled edges with right sides facing and stitch to the outside point as shown in Figure 4. Press seams to one side. This completes a block. Make 20 blocks in this way.

To join blocks

1. With right sides facing, stitch the right side edge of one block to the left side edge of another block.

2. Continue to join 5 blocks in this way to make a row, as shown in Figure 5. Press seams to one side. Make 5 rows in this way.

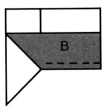

Figure 3

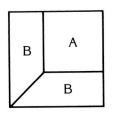

Figure 4

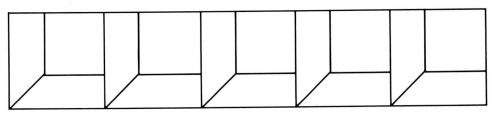

Figure 5

To join rows

Refer to the assembly diagram.

1. With right sides facing, stitch the bottom edge of the first row to the top edge of the second row.

2. Continue to join all 5 rows in this way to make the top piece of the wall hanging.

To quilt

1. With wrong sides facing, pin the pieced top, batting, and backing together.

Tip: I usually recommend quilting ¼ inch on each side of all seam lines when you are working on a larger project. When the seams are so close together, such as on a project this small, the stitching looks better when it's closer together.

To finish

1. When all quilting has been completed, remove the pins.

2. Trim the batting to ½ inch smaller than the quilt top all around.

3. Turn the raw edges of the backing piece to the inside ¼ inch all around and press.

4. Turn each edge over again onto the front of the wall hanging to create a ½-inch border.

5. Slip-stitch the edge to the front of the fabric.

6. Arrange a few stars and the moon in the upper right-hand blocks on the dark squares. Stitch or glue them in place.

7. The added lines on the assembly diagram represent the rays from the moon. Using the silver thread and the illustration for placement, backstitch these lines.

To hang

Attach Velcro® tabs to the back of each top corner and in the center. Attach corresponding tabs to the wall where the wall hanging will go.

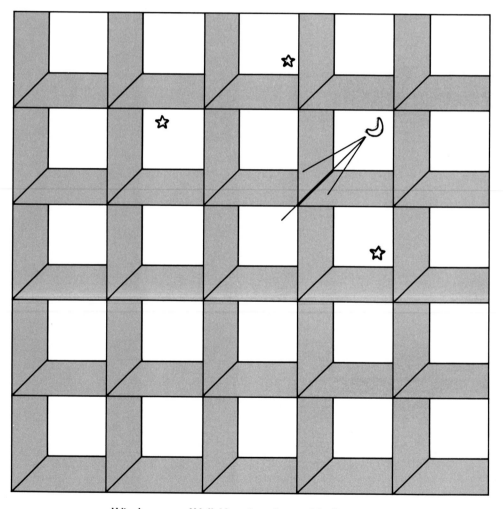

Windowpane Wall Hanging Assembly Diagram

WINDOWPANE WALL HANGING TEMPLATES

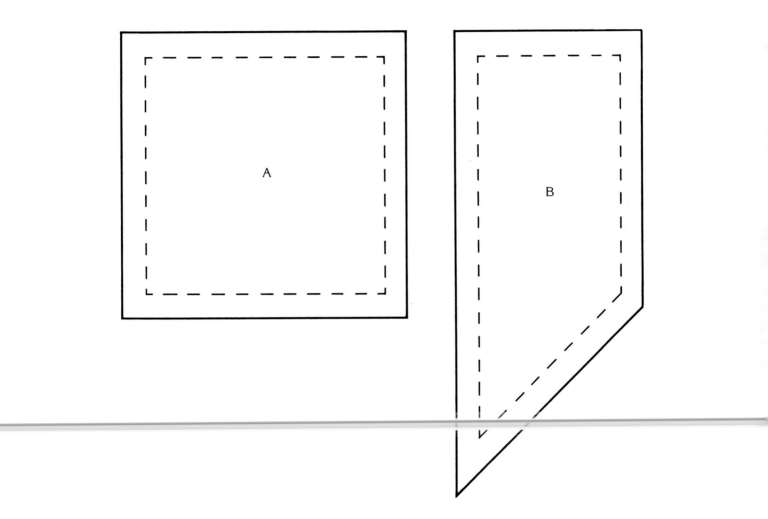

Road to St. Louis Quilt

Kate McCombe of Nantucket Island used assorted calicos and solids to make this pretty wall hanging, which looks more complicated than it is. The pattern is easy to reproduce as it is created from simple triangles and squares. The finished project measures 46 × 58 inches and would make an ample throw or a single bed cover. If you'd like to enlarge the size, simply add a wider border all around.

Materials

Note: All yardages are figured for 45-inch-wide fabric. Since the quilt is 46 inches wide, you will have to piece the backing fabric (see page 12 for instructions). If you prefer one solid piece for the back, you can use a single sheet or you will need 60-inch-wide fabric. Muslin comes wider than most fabrics and is often used to back quilts and wall hangings.

   1¾ yards cream print
   1¾ yards brown print
   1¾ yards backing fabric
   ⅛ yard each of 8–10 assorted calicos and solids
   quilt batting
   tracing paper
   cardboard

Cutting List

Note: All measurements include a ¼-inch seam allowance, except for backing pieces, which include a ½-inch seam allowance.

Tip: When you have several strips of fabric in different colors, it's a good idea to mark the back of each one after cutting.

Trace patterns A, B, and C and transfer to cardboard for templates (see page 11). Place the patterns on the back of the appropriate fabrics as indicated on the next page.

43

Cut the following:

from cream print:
    2 strips, each 1½ × 58½ inches
      (outer side borders)
    2 strips, each 1½ × 44½ inches
      (outer top and bottom
      borders)
    2 strips, each 1 × 52½ inches
      (inner side borders)
    2 strips, each 1 × 39½ inches
      (inner top and bottom
      borders)
    28 - B
    34 - C

from brown print:
    2 strips, each 2½ × 56½ inches
      (outer side borders)

    2 strips, each 2½ × 40½ inches
      (outer top and bottom
      borders)
    2 strips, each 2 × 51½ inches
      (inner side borders)
    2 strips, each 2 × 36½ inches
      (inner top and bottom
      borders)

from backing fabric:
    1 piece 47 × 59 inches; or 1
      piece 24 × 59 inches, and 2
      pieces, 12½ × 59 inches

from all solids and calicos (try to evenly distribute pieces to be cut):
    384 - A

Figure 1

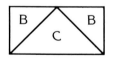

Figure 2

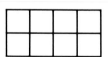

Figure 3

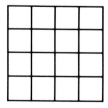

Figure 4

Directions

Block 1 Refer to Figure 1.

1. With right sides facing, stitch 2 A pieces together to make a row. Make 2 rows in this way. Press seams to one side.

2. With right sides facing, stitch these 2 rows together to make a block of 4 squares. Make 4 of Block 1. Press seams to one side.

Block 2 Refer to Figure 2.

1. With right sides facing, stitch 4 A pieces together to make a row. Make 2 rows in this way. Press seams to one side.

2. With right sides facing, stitch the bottom edge of one row to the top edge of the other row. Press seams to one side. Make 10 of Block 2.

Block 3 Refer to Figure 3.

1. With right sides facing, stitch the diagonal side of a cream B piece to one short side of a brown C piece.

2. Repeat with another cream B piece to the other short side of the brown C piece. Press seams to one side. Make 14 of Block 3.

Block 4 Refer to Figure 4.

1. With right sides facing, stitch 4 A pieces together to make a row. Make 4 rows in this way. Press seams to one side.

2. Next, stitch the 4 rows together to make a block. Press seams to one side. Make 18 of Block 4.

Block 5 Refer to Figure 5.

1. With right sides facing, stitch one short side of a brown C piece to one short side of a cream C piece to make a larger triangle. Make 2 large triangles in this way. Press seams to one side.

2. Next, stitch the 2 large triangles together along the diagonal to make a block. Press seams to one side. Make 17 of Block 5.

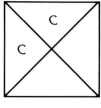

Figure 5

To make rows

1. See Figure 6. With right sides facing, stitch the right side of Block 1 to the left short side of Block 3. Next, stitch the other short side of Block 3 to one short side of Block 2.

2. Continue in this way with another Block 3, then Block 2, followed by another Block 3, and end the row with another Block 1. Press seams to one side. Make 2 rows in this way for Rows 1 and 9.

3. See Figure 7. With right sides facing, stitch the long brown edge of Block 3 to one side edge of Block 4. Next, stitch the other side of Block 4 to one brown side of Block 5.

4. Continue in this way with another Block 4, Block 5, Block 4, and end the row with another Block 3. Press seams to one side. Make 4 rows in this way for Rows 2, 4, 6, and 8.

5. See Figure 8. With right sides facing, stitch one long edge of Block 2 to one cream side of Block 5. Stitch the other cream side of Block 5 to one side of Block 4.

6. Continue in this way with another Block 5, Block 4, Block 5, and end with another Block 2. Press seams to one side. Make 3 rows in this way for Rows 3, 5, and 7.

Figure 6

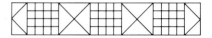

Figure 7

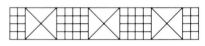

Figure 8

To join rows

Refer to the assembly diagram.

1. With right sides facing, stitch the bottom edge of Row 1 to the top edge of Row 2. Press seams to one side.

2. Next, stitch the bottom edge of Row 2 to the top edge of Row 3.

3. Continue to join all 9 rows in this way. Press seams to one side.

To add borders

Refer to the assembly diagram.

1. With right sides facing, stitch the short brown strips (2 × 36½ inches) to the top and bottom edges of the quilt top. Press seams to one side.

2. Next, stitch the 2 × 51½-inch brown strips to the sides in the same way.

3. With right sides facing, stitch the 1 × 39½-inch cream strips to the top and bottom edges of the quilt top. Press seams to one side.

4. Stitch the 1 × 52½-inch cream strips to the sides in the same way.

5. With right sides facing, stitch the 2½ × 40½-inch brown strips to the top and bottom edges and the remaining 2½ × 56½-inch brown strips to the sides. Press seams to one side.

45

6. With right sides facing, stitch the 1½ × 44½-inch cream strips to the top and bottom edges and the remaining 1½ × 58½-inch cream strips to the side edges. Press seams to one side.

To quilt

1. Cut or piece the backing fabric so it's slightly larger than the quilt top all around.
2. With wrong sides facing, pin the top, batting, and backing together.
3. Starting at the center and working outward in a sunburst pattern, take long, loose basting stitches through all 3 layers (see page 14).
4. Take small running stitches on each side of all seam lines, stopping ½ inch from the outer edges.

To finish

1. When all quilting has been completed, remove basting stitches.
2. Trim the batting ½ inch smaller than the quilt top all around. Trim the backing fabric to the same size as the quilt top.
3. Turn the raw edges of the backing and the quilt top to the inside ½ inch and press. Machine- or slip-stitch all around.

Road to St. Louis Quilt
Assembly Diagram

Row 1
Row 2
Row 3
Row 4
Row 5
Row 6
Row 7
Row 8
Row 9

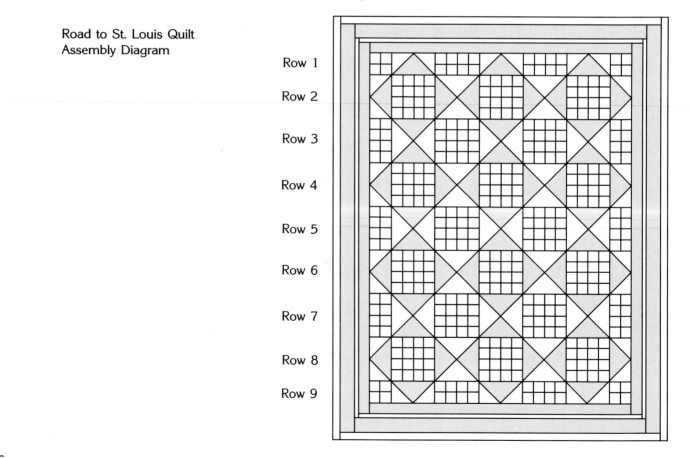

ROAD TO ST. LOUIS QUILT TEMPLATES

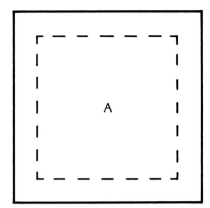

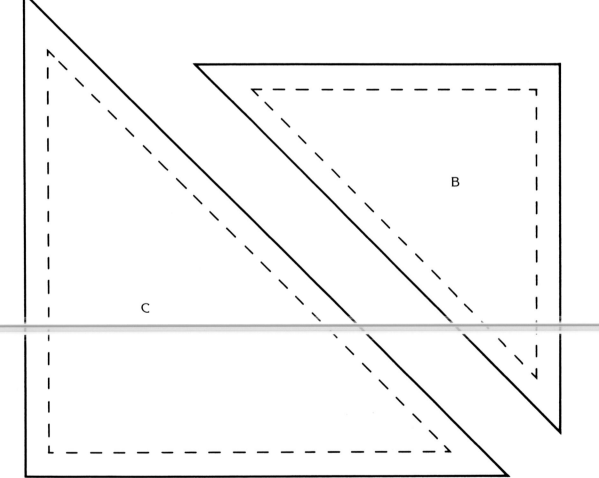

47

Birdhouse Wall Hanging

A small appliquéd wall hanging is nice for adding a decorative touch to any room. Hand-quilting around the appliqué makes the design stand out and holds all layers of fabric together. The finished size is 13 × 13 inches. If you'd like the project to be larger, simply add another border all around.

Materials

    small pieces of green and light blue solids
    small pieces of yellow calico and navy blue calico
    scraps of red calico and pink solid
    backing fabric piece 14 × 14 inches
    thin quilt batting 14 × 14 inches
    fusible webbing
    tracing paper
    thin cardboard
    2 small curtain rings or 2 small Velcro® tabs for hanging

Cutting List

Note: All measurements include a ¼-inch seam allowance.

Trace triangle A and transfer to cardboard for template (see page 11).

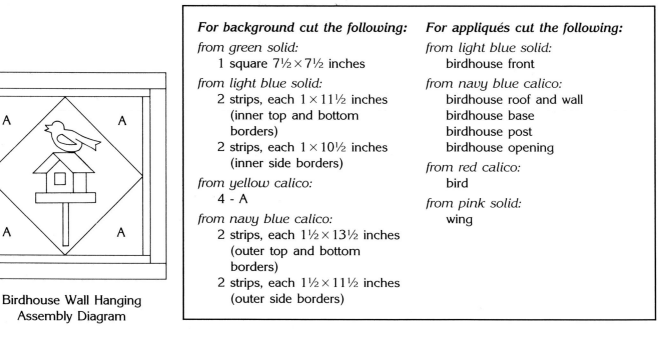

Birdhouse Wall Hanging
Assembly Diagram

For background cut the following:	For appliqués cut the following:

from green solid:
    1 square 7½ × 7½ inches
	from light blue solid:
	    birdhouse front

from light blue solid:
    2 strips, each 1 × 11½ inches
    (inner top and bottom
    borders)
    2 strips, each 1 × 10½ inches
    (inner side borders)
	from navy blue calico:
	    birdhouse roof and wall
	    birdhouse base
	    birdhouse post
	    birdhouse opening

from yellow calico:
    4 - A
	from red calico:
	    bird

from navy blue calico:
    2 strips, each 1½ × 13½ inches
    (outer top and bottom
    borders)
    2 strips, each 1½ × 11½ inches
    (outer side borders)
	from pink solid:
	    wing

Directions

To prepare appliqué

1. Trace each pattern piece and pin it to the right side of each fabric as indicated.
2. Pin a piece of fusible webbing to the wrong side of each piece and cut out.
3. Trace the entire design to use as a placement guide. Center the tracing on the green square and arrange each appliqué piece under the tracing. Remove the tracing and fuse each piece to the background with a medium-hot iron.

To piece background and borders

Refer to the assembly diagram.

1. With right sides facing, stitch the long, diagonal side of each yellow calico A piece to each side of the green solid square. Open seams and press.
2. With right sides facing, stitch the $1 \times 10\frac{1}{2}$-inch light blue strips to each side of the square.
3. Next, stitch the $1 \times 11\frac{1}{2}$-inch light blue strips to the top and bottom edges. Open seams and press.
4. With right sides facing, stitch the $1\frac{1}{2} \times 11\frac{1}{2}$-inch navy blue calico strips to each side of this square. Next, stitch the $1\frac{1}{2} \times 13\frac{1}{2}$-inch navy blue calico strips to the top and bottom edges. Open seams and press.
5. Trace the corner quilting pattern and transfer it to each yellow calico piece (see page 13).

To quilt

1. Cut the quilt batting the same size as the backing piece.
2. With wrong sides facing, pin the top, the batting, and the backing together.
3. The dotted lines on the assembly diagram and the appliqué patterns represent the quilting lines. Use small running stitches to quilt along the outside edge of each fused appliqué. For added interest, quilt $\frac{1}{4}$ inch on the outside of the first quilting stitches and on each side of the seam lines. Quilt each corner pattern with small running stitches. (See hand-quilting instructions on page 14.)

To finish

1. When all quilting has been completed, remove all pins.
2. Trim the batting to $\frac{1}{4}$ inch smaller than the top piece all around.
3. Trim backing to same size as top.
4. Turn the raw edges of the top piece and the raw edges of the backing to the inside $\frac{1}{4}$ inch on each side and press.
5. Slip-stitch or machine-stitch as close to the edge as possible all around.
6. Attach a small curtain ring to the back at each top corner or add small Velcro® tabs for hanging.

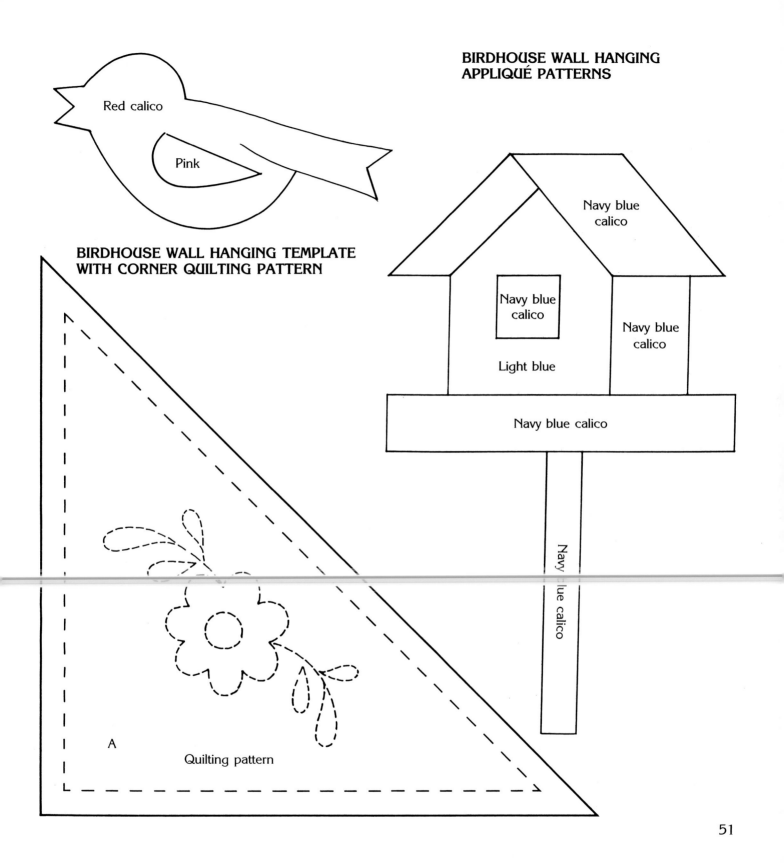

BIRDHOUSE WALL HANGING
APPLIQUÉ PATTERNS

Red calico

Pink

BIRDHOUSE WALL HANGING TEMPLATE
WITH CORNER QUILTING PATTERN

Navy blue
calico

Navy blue
calico

Navy blue
calico

Light blue

Navy blue calico

Navy blue calico

A

Quilting pattern

51

Pastel Baby Quilt

Pastel squares divided by lattice strips of white create a cheerful but soft design for a baby quilt. It's easy to make and fun to give. You might like to use these directions but substitute bright colors or colors to match the baby's room. The finished size is 40 × 46 inches and will fit a standard crib.

Materials

Note: All yardages are figured for 45-inch-wide fabric.

> 1½ yards yellow gingham
> 1½ yards backing fabric
> ¾ yard white solid
> ⅛ yard each of cream (A), blue (B), light green (C), pink (D), and yellow (E) solids
> cotton quilt batting 40 × 46 inches
> tracing paper
> cardboard

Cutting List

Note: All measurements include a ¼-inch seam allowance.

Trace the square pattern and transfer to cardboard to make a template (see page 11). Use the template to cut all squares of fabric.

Cut the following:

from yellow gingham:
- 2 strips, each 4½ × 46½ inches (side borders)
- 2 strips, each 4½ × 32½ inches (top and bottom borders)

from backing fabric:
- 1 piece 41 × 47 inches

from white solid:
- 24 lattice strips, each 2½ × 4½ inches

- 7 lattice strips, each 2½ × 28½ inches
- 2 lattice strips, each 2½ × 38½ inches

from each of cream (A), blue (B), light green (C), pink (D), and yellow (E) solids:
- 6 squares

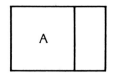

Figure 1

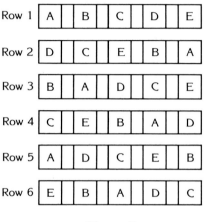

Row 1	A		B		C		D		E
Row 2	D		C		E		B		A
Row 3	B		A		D		C		E
Row 4	C		E		B		A		D
Row 5	A		D		C		E		B
Row 6	E		B		A		D		C

Figure 2

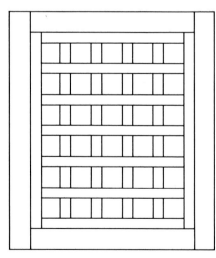

Pastel Baby Quilt
Assembly Diagram

Directions

To make a row

1. With right sides facing and raw edges aligned, stitch a $2\frac{1}{2} \times 4\frac{1}{2}$-inch white lattice strip to the right side of a cream (A) square, as shown in Figure 1. Press seams to one side.

2. Refer to Figure 2. Next, join a blue (B) square. Continue with another $2\frac{1}{2} \times 4\frac{1}{2}$-inch white lattice strip, a green (C) square, another short lattice strip, a pink (D) square, another short lattice strip, and end with a yellow (E) square to make a row of 5 squares separated by 4 short lattice strips. Press seams to one side.

3. Refer to the following color sequence and Figure 2 to make 5 more rows.

    Row 2: D C E B A
    Row 3: B A D C E
    Row 4: C E B A D
    Row 5: A D C E B
    Row 6: E B A D C

To join rows

Refer to the assembly diagram.

1. With right sides facing, stitch a $2\frac{1}{2} \times 28$-inch white lattice strip to the top edge of Row 1. Press seams to one side.

2. Join another lattice strip of the same size to the bottom edge of Row 1. Continue to join all 6 rows separated by $2\frac{1}{2} \times 28$-inch white lattice strips in this way, ending with a lattice strip along the bottom edge.

3. Stitch a $2\frac{1}{2} \times 38\frac{1}{2}$-inch white lattice strip to each side of the joined rows. Press seams to one side.

To make borders

Refer to the assembly diagram.

1. With right sides facing, stitch $4\frac{1}{2} \times 32\frac{1}{2}$-inch yellow calico border strips to the top and bottom edges of the quilt top. Press seams to one side.

2. Stitch the $4\frac{1}{2} \times 46\frac{1}{2}$-inch yellow gingham strips to the sides in the same way. Press seams to one side.

To quilt

1. Center the batting on the wrong side of the backing fabric. Next, place the quilt top right side up on the batting and pin all 3 layers together.

2. Beginning at the center of the quilt and working outward, baste all 3 layers together with long stitches in a sunburst pattern (see page 14).

3. By hand: Take small running stitches on each side of all seam lines through all 3 layers. By machine: Stitch in the channel of all seam lines.

Stop stitches ½ inch from the edge of the quilt all around. Do not stitch into outside seam allowance.

4. Remove basting stitches. Trim the batting ½ inch smaller than the quilt top all around. Trim the backing to the same size as the quilt top.

To finish
Turn the raw edges of the quilt top and backing to the inside ¼ inch and press. Slip-stitch or machine-stitch all around to close.

PASTEL BABY QUILT TEMPLATE

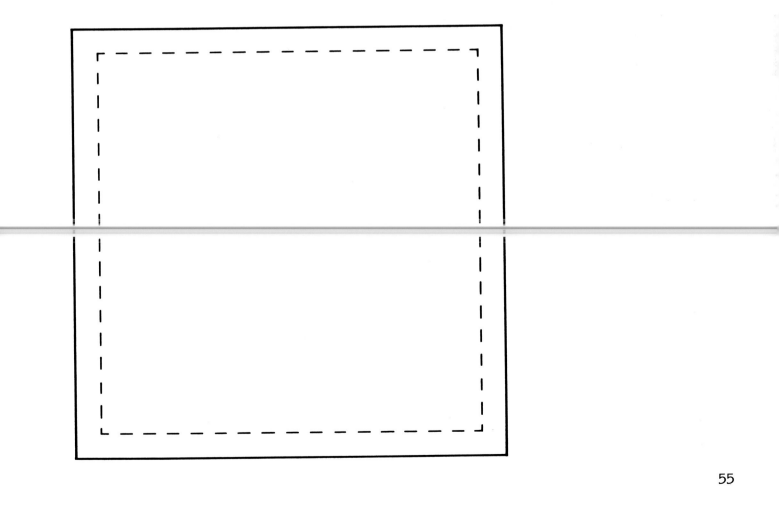

Toy Boat Appliqué

Use scraps of fabric to create a delightful wall hanging for a child's room. The design is made as a block and could be used for a pillow or a small crib quilt. The finished wall hanging is 11×11 inches.

Materials

small pieces of light blue solid, green solid, and blue calico
scraps of yellow, red, blue, black, and white solids
thin quilt batting 12×12 inches
fusible webbing
bias binding or frame (optional)
Velcro® tabs for hanging (optional)

Cutting List

Note: Background pieces include a ¼-inch seam allowance. Appliqué pieces do not include any seam allowance (and you should not add any as you cut) because pieces are fused to the background with fusible webbing.

Tip: As you cut each background piece, identify it on the back in pencil.

Trace each appliqué pattern piece from the book and cut it out. Pin each pattern piece to the right side of the corresponding fabric and then to fusible webbing.

For background cut the following:	*For appliqué cut the following:*

from light blue solid:
    1 piece 7½ × 9½ inches
	from yellow solid:
	    1 - A
	    1 - B

from green solid:
    1 piece 2½ × 9½ inches
	from red solid:
	    1 - C

from blue calico:
    4 strips, each 1½ × 9½ inches
	from blue solid:
	    1 - D

from black solid:
    4 squares, each 1½ × 1½ inches
	from black solid:
	    2 - E
	    1 - F

	from white solid: 1 - G

Directions

To make the background

1. With right sides facing, stitch the bottom long edge of the light blue piece to the top long edge of the green piece to make a 9½-inch square. This represents the sky and water. Open the seams and press.

2. Next, stitch a blue calico strip to each side of this square. Press the seams open.

3. With right sides facing, stitch a black square to each short end of the remaining 2 strips.

4. Join these strips to the top and bottom of the background square. Open the seams and press.

To appliqué

1. Position and pin each pattern piece on the fabric as indicated in the photograph. Tuck the bottom edges of red C and yellow B under the top edge of the blue boat D as shown. Position and pin black F and white G.

2. Using a medium-hot iron, fuse each piece in place.

3. Place yellow A on top of the blue boat just above the seam line of the background and pin. Position and pin the 2 black E pieces on top of yellow B. Fuse the pieces in place.

4. Use matching thread and a narrow zigzag stitch to attach each pattern piece to the background material.

To quilt

1. Trace the sun pattern and transfer it to the upper left-hand corner of the sky (see page 13).

2. Pin the appliquéd block to the thin quilt batting. Using small running stitches, hand-quilt along the marked sun lines (see page 14).

To finish

You can either frame this in a standard frame or finish the edges with bias binding and attach to the wall with Velcro® tabs. Turn raw edges under ¼ inch and press. Machine-stitch all around.

58

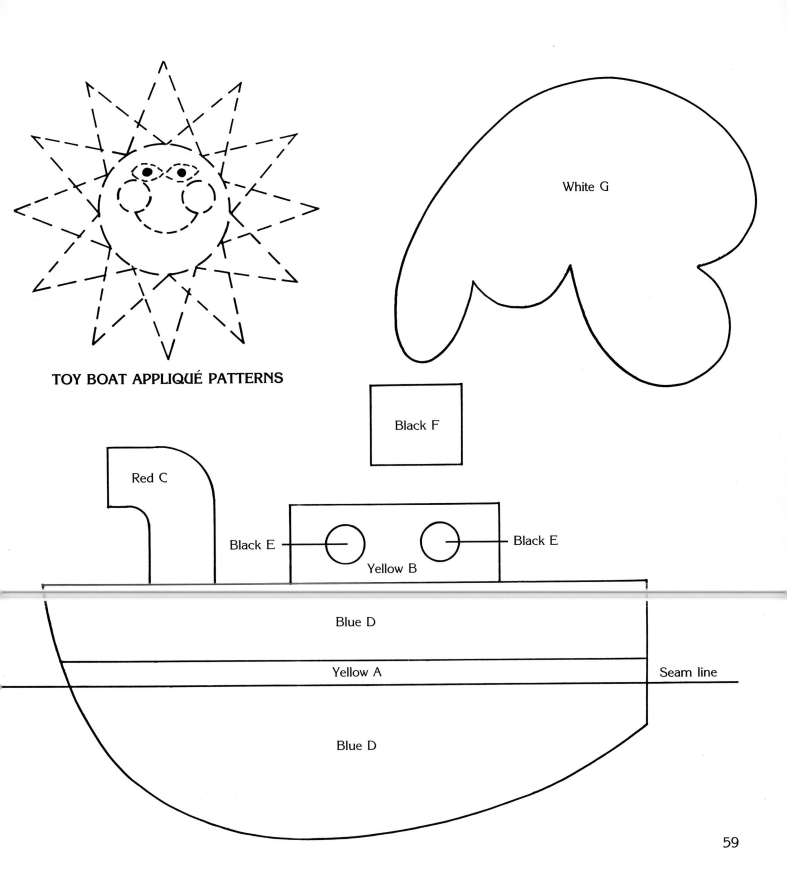

TOY BOAT APPLIQUÉ PATTERNS

White G

Black F

Red C

Black E — Black E
Yellow B

Blue D

Yellow A   Seam line

Blue D

59

Sherbet Crib Quilt

A crib-sized quilt is always a pleasure to make. It's manageable and easy to quilt in your lap. Many experienced quilters who have made quite elaborate quilt patterns are enjoying the experience of making small quilts. These projects can be completed more quickly and make the most wonderful gifts. No matter how many times you wash a baby quilt, it looks better and better. This one, which is 32 × 44 inches, would make a nice wall hanging as well. We used thin quilt batting, but if you want a puffier quilt, use a traditional loft. My mother, Ruth Linsley, pieced and quilted this project.

Materials

Note: All yardages are figured for 45-inch-wide fabric.

    1 yard backing fabric
    ½ yard white solid
    ½ yard light green calico for borders
    ¼ yard each of blue, raspberry, purple, pink, yellow, and green solids
    1 yard quilt batting
    tracing paper

Cutting List

Note: All measurements include a ¼-inch seam allowance.

Trace the triangle and transfer to cardboard for template (see page 11).

Cut the following:

from backing fabric:
    1 piece 33 × 45 inches

from white solid:
    54 triangles

from light green calico:
    2 strips, each 4½ × 36½ inches
    (side borders)

    2 strips, each 4½ × 32½ inches
    (top and bottom borders)

from each of blue, raspberry, purple, pink, yellow, and green solids:
    9 triangles

Directions

To make squares

1. With right sides facing, stitch a blue triangle to a white triangle along the diagonal to make a square. Press seams to the blue side. Make 9 squares in this way (see Figure 1).

Figure 1

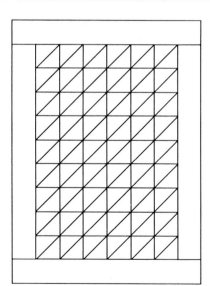

Figure 2

2. Continue to stitch the 9 triangles of each color to the white triangles to make 9 squares of each color with white for a total of 54 squares. Press seams to color side.

To make a block

Note: Each block uses 9 squares of the same color.

1. With right sides facing, stitch 2 squares together. Continue with another square to make a row of 3 squares.

2. Make 3 rows of 3 squares each. Press all seams to the dark side.

3. With right sides facing, stitch all 3 rows together to make a block, as shown in Figure 2. Press seams to dark side.

4. Make 1 block of each color for a total of 6 blocks.

To make quilt top

Refer to the assembly diagram.

1. With right sides facing and seams matching, stitch the blue/white block to the raspberry/white block. This is the top row of the quilt as shown.

2. Next, stitch the purple/white block to the pink/white block for the center row and stitch the yellow/white block to the green/white block for the bottom row of the quilt. Press seams to one side.

3. With right sides facing and seams matching, stitch all 3 rows together. Press seams to one side.

4. With right sides facing, attach a 4½ × 36½-inch green calico border strip to each side of the quilt top. Stitch the remaining 4½ × 32½-inch green calico border strips to the top and bottom edges of the quilt top. Press seams to one side.

To mark quilting lines

See page 13 for instructions on transferring a design.

1. Trace the sun ray quilting pattern and transfer it to each corner of the border.

2. Trace the swirling quilting pattern and transfer it to the top, bottom, and side borders.

Tip: For a simpler quilting pattern, use a yardstick to mark a diagonal grid across the borders (see page 14).

To quilt

1. With wrong sides facing, pin quilt top, batting, and backing together.

2. Beginning at the center of the quilt and working to the outer edges, take long, loose basting stitches through all 3 layers in a sunburst pattern (see page 14).

3. Using small running stitches, quilt ¼ inch on each side of all seam lines in the blocks and along all premarked quilting lines in the borders, stopping ½ inch from the edges all around the quilt.

Sherbet Crib Quilt
Assembly Diagram

To finish

1. When all quilting has been completed, remove basting stitches.

2. Trim the batting to ½ inch smaller than the quilt top all around. Next, trim the backing fabric to the same size as the quilt top.

3. Turn the raw edges of the quilt top and backing fabric to the inside ¼ inch on each side and press.

4. Pin together and then machine- or slip-stitch all around.

SHERBET CRIB QUILT TEMPLATE

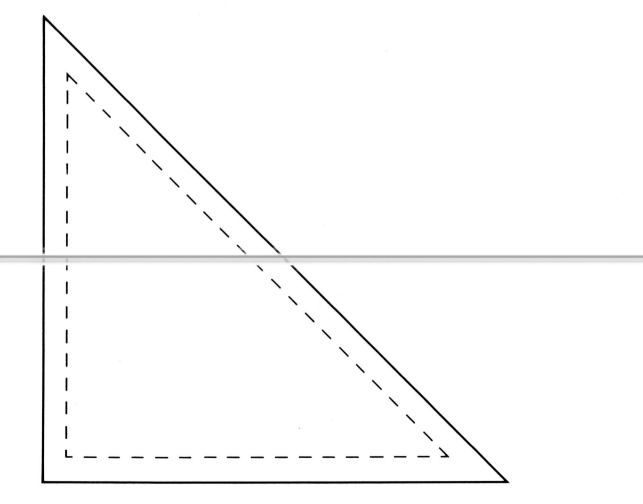

63

QUILTING PATTERNS

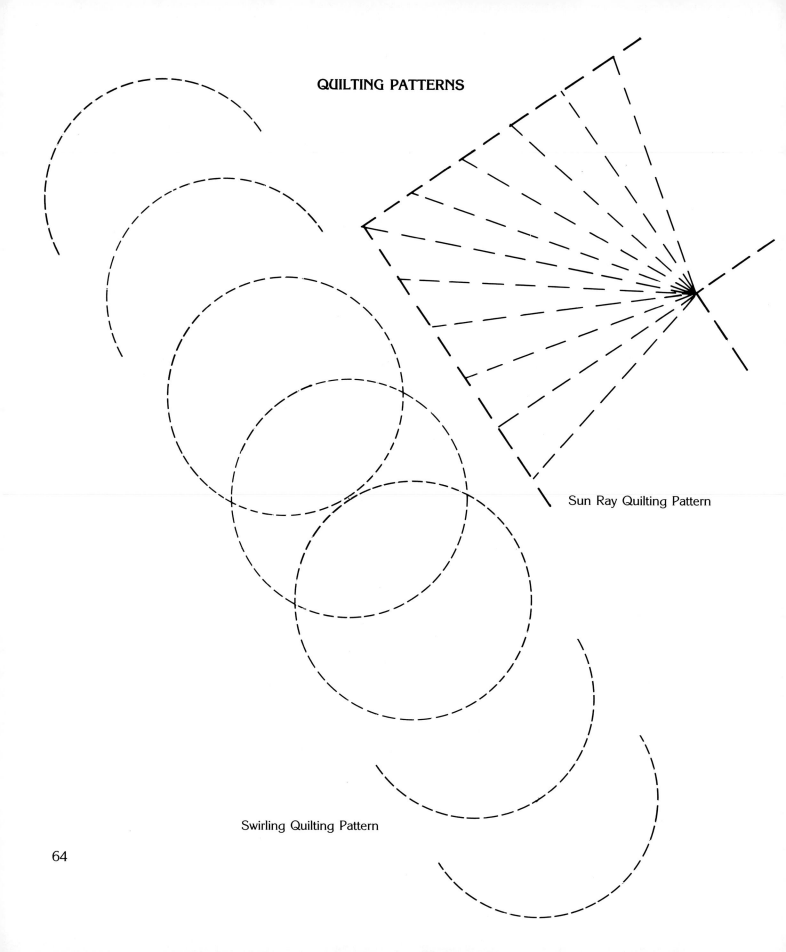

Sun Ray Quilting Pattern

Swirling Quilting Pattern

64

Taxi Cab Wall Hanging

Make this yellow-and-black appliqué wall hanging to brighten a young child's room. Since the design is made in blocks, you can easily expand this project into a bed-sized quilt by adding more blocks across and more rows down, and by finishing with wide borders. It would make a snappy quilt to match the wall hanging, which is 21½ × 27½ inches.

Materials

Note: All yardages are figured for 45-inch-wide fabric.

Tip: Since the appliqués are made of light colors over a black background, you might want to use a heavier-weight fabric, such as canvas, or consider adding a lining to cotton fabric.

    1 yard black calico (includes backing)
    ½ yard yellow solid
    small piece of white solid
    quilt batting
    tracing paper
    thin cardboard
    Velcro® tabs for hanging

Cutting List

Note: All measurements include a ¼-inch seam allowance.

Trace the outer line of the taxi cab and wheel patterns and transfer to cardboard for templates (see page 11). These include a ¼-inch seam allowance. Trace around the inside line of each pattern and transfer to card-board for templates. These are the actual size.

Cut the following:

from black calico:
    4 rectangles, each 8 × 11 inches
    2 strips, each 2 × 22 inches
        (outer top and bottom
        borders)
    3 strips, each 2 × 16 inches
        (outer side borders)
    1 backing piece 22 × 28 inches

from yellow solid:
    4 taxi cab appliqués
    2 lattice strips, each 1 × 8 inches
    1 lattice strip 1 × 22 inches
    2 border strips, each 2 × 22
        inches (inner top and bottom
        borders)
    3 strips, each 2 × 16 inches
        (inner side borders)

from white solid:
    8 wheel appliqués

Directions

To prepare appliqué pieces

1. Using the yellow solid fabric, trace around the larger taxi template 4 times and cut each one out. Center the smaller taxi template on one of the larger outlines so there is ¼ inch of fabric all around.
2. Fold the seam allowance over the template, clipping into the seam allowance around the curves and pressing as you do this, as shown in Figure 1.
3. Remove the template and use it again for the 3 remaining taxi pieces.
4. Using the white fabric, trace around the larger wheel template 8 times. Cut out each wheel ⅛ inch larger than the marked line all around. Since it is difficult to turn the seam allowance under to make a round circle, use the following method, shown in Figure 2: Baste-stitch along the marked line, leaving about 2 inches of extra thread at the end. Center the smaller wheel template on the fabric wheel and pull on the end of the basting thread. This will gather the seam allowance around the template. Remove the template and press the fabric.
5. Make 8 wheels in this way.

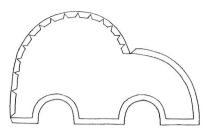

Figure 1

To appliqué

Refer to the assembly diagram.

1. Center each taxi cab on a black rectangle and pin in place.
2. Using matching thread, machine-stitch close to the edge of the appliqué all around.
3. Next, arrange the wheels, leaving a ¼-inch space between the taxi and the wheels as shown in the assembly diagram. Pin each one in place.
4. Using matching thread, stitch around each wheel close to the edge.

Note: It may be difficult to make such a small turn on your sewing machine. Take a few stitches; then, leaving the needle in the fabric, lift your pressure foot and turn the fabric slightly. Replace the pressure foot and continue in this way all around. If you prefer to hand-appliqué, blind- or whipstitch around each piece (see page 10).

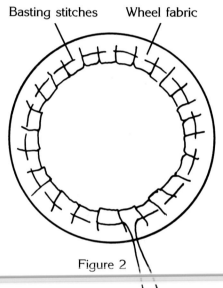

Basting stitches   Wheel fabric

Figure 2

To assemble wall hanging

Refer to the assembly diagram.

1. With right sides facing, stitch one 1 × 8-inch yellow lattice strip to the right side of one taxi cab block. Next, stitch this to another block for the top row. Press seams to the dark side.
2. Make the bottom row in the same way.
3. With right sides facing, stitch the 1 × 22-inch yellow lattice strip to the bottom edge of the top row. Open and press seams to one side.
4. With right sides facing, join this to the top edge of the bottom row. Open and press seams to one side.

Taxi Cab Wall Hanging Assembly Diagram

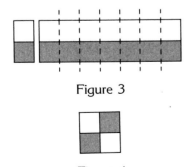

Figure 3

Figure 4

5. With right sides facing, stitch a 2 × 16-inch yellow border strip to a 2 × 16-inch black calico border strip along one long edge. Make 3 sets of 2 × 16-inch yellow and black border strips.

6. Measure and mark one of these sets into 2-inch sections and cut as shown in Figure 3. You will have 8 sections of yellow and black squares. Next, stitch 2 of these sections together to make a square as shown in Figure 4. Make 3 more squares. These are the corner blocks.

7. With right sides facing, stitch a 2 × 22-inch yellow border strip to a 2 × 22-inch black calico border strip along one long edge. Make 2. Press seams to one side.

8. With right sides facing and seams matching, stitch a corner block to each short end of the two 22-inch-long border pieces.

9. With right sides facing, stitch the short border section to each side of the quilt top. Press seams to one side.

10. Refer to the assembly diagram and stitch the 22-inch-long border sections with the corner blocks to the top and bottom of the quilt top so that the yellow is on the inside. Press seams to one side.

To quilt

1. With wrong sides facing, pin the top, batting, and backing together.

2. Using small running stitches, quilt ¼ inch on each side of all seam lines, stopping ¾ inch from the outside edges all around.

To finish

1. When all quilting has been completed, remove all pins.

2. Trim the batting ¼ inch smaller than the quilt top. Trim the backing fabric to the same size as the quilt top.

3. Turn the raw edges of the top and backing to the inside ¼ inch and press. Pin all around.

4. Slip-stitch around the edges to close.

To hang

Attach Velcro® tabs to the back of each corner of the hanging. Add another tab to the back of the center of the top and bottom edges. Attach corresponding tabs to the wall and attach quilt hanging.

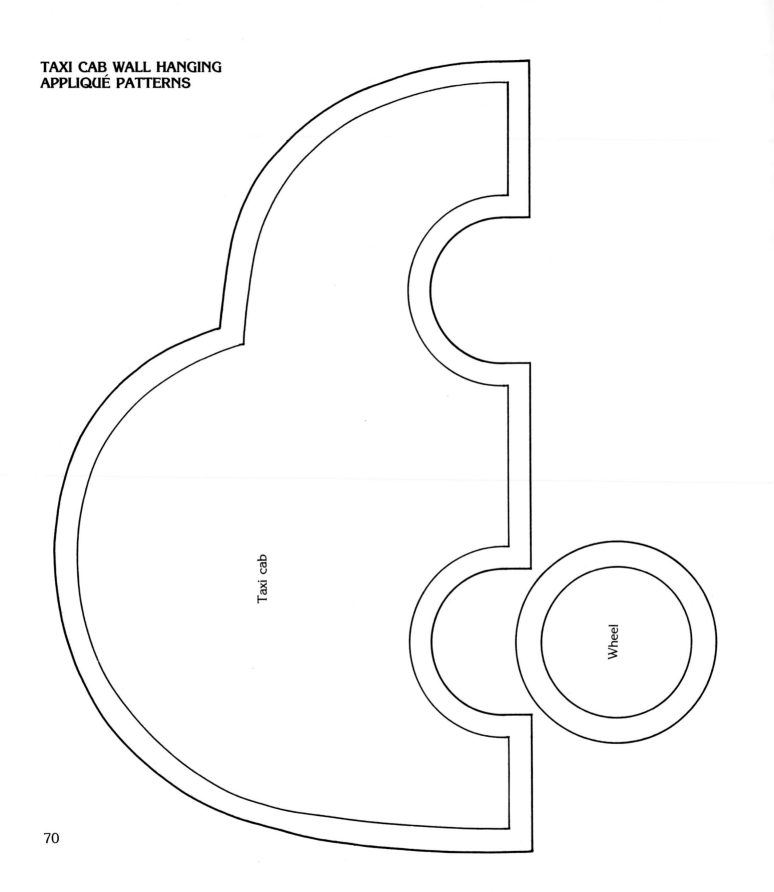

Taxi cab

Wheel

Her First Dolly

This soft little doll is made of muslin with yarn for hair. She measures 11 inches high and is perfect for a first dolly. Her dress and apron are removable and trimmed with lace and heart appliqués.

Materials

Note: All yardages are figured for 45-inch-wide fabric.

½ yard unbleached muslin
⅛ yard mint green calico
small amount of blue and red embroidery floss for eyes and mouth
embroidery needle
stuffing
1 yard ½-inch-wide lace
12 inches thin elastic
2½-inch strip of Velcro® or small snaps for dress clothing
1 skein yellow knitting yarn
craft glue (optional to attach hair)
1 yard thin satin ribbon

Cutting List

Note: All measurements include a ¼-inch seam allowance.

Trace patterns A, B, C, D, and E and cut out.

Cut the following:	*from mint green calico:*
from muslin:	4 foot C (cut 2 of them in reverse)
2 head/body A	1
4 leg B (cut 2 of them in reverse)	1 dress top D
1 piece 2½×9 inches (apron)	2 heart appliqué E
1 strip 1×21 inches (waistband/ties)	1 piece 3×26 inches (dress skirt)

Directions

To prepare doll body

1. Transfer the pattern for the facial features to the right side of one head/body piece (see page 13).

2. Using 2 strands of blue embroidery floss, backstitch to outline the eyes.

Use the satin stitch to fill in the eyes. Using 2 strands of red floss, outline the mouth. (See the embroidery stitches on page 74.)

3. With right sides facing, stitch the 2 head/body pieces together, leaving the bottom edge open.

4. With right sides facing, stitch each B (leg) piece to a C (foot) piece. Press seams to one side. Next, stitch 2 matching leg/foot pieces together, leaving the top edges open. Make 2.

5. Clip all curves and turn all pieces right side out. Press.

To assemble doll Refer to Figure 1.

1. Stuff the arms. Stitch across the broken line to close the arms.

2. Stuff each leg and the head/body piece. Turn the raw edges of the body to the inside ¼ inch and stitch across to close the body.

3. Turn the raw edges of each leg piece to the inside ¼ inch. With the leg seams centered in the front and back, stitch across to attach each leg to the bottom edge of the body.

Seam — — Seam

Figure 1

To make dress Refer to Figure 2.

1. With right sides facing, fold the top dress piece in half on the fold line. Pin together and stitch under each sleeve and down each side.

2. Cut the back open in the center from the neck to the bottom edge.

3. Turn the raw edges of the neck, sleeves, and back opening under ⅛ inch and press. Turn under again ⅛ inch and press.

4. Cut the elastic in half and stitch one piece around the inside of each sleeve at the hemline.

5. Cut a piece of lace to go around the neckline and stitch to the inside of the neck at the hemline.

6. Turn the bottom long edge of the skirt under ⅛ inch and press. Turn under another ⅛ inch and stitch the raw edge of the remaining strip of lace to the underside.

7. With right sides facing, fold the skirt in half and stitch along the short ends.

8. With right sides facing, pin the top and bottom of the dress together, gathering the skirt to fit as you do this. Turn the skirt right side out and press. Turn the bottom edge under ⅛ inch, press, and turn under another ⅛ inch. Attach a lace trim all around as you stitch the hem.

9. Attach the strip of Velcro® or small snaps to the back opening of the dress. If you are using snaps, stitch along the seam line of the opening to finish it before attaching snaps.

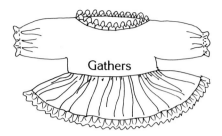

Figure 2

To make apron Refer to Figure 3.

1. Turn the bottom edge and sides of the apron under ⅛ inch and press.

2. Pin a calico heart to each side of the apron front and zigzag-stitch around the raw edges.

3. Turn each long edge and the ends of the waistband and ties under ¼ inch and press. Next, fold in half lengthwise and press.

4. Gather the top raw edges of the apron so it measures 6 inches across and pin between the fold of the waistband. Stitch across the folded edge of the waistband with the raw edge of the apron inside.

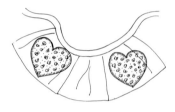

Figure 3

5. Tie the apron on the doll over the dress.

To attach hair Refer to Figure 4.

1. Cut approximately 100 strands of 12-inch-long yarn.

2. Cut a narrow strip of fabric 5 inches long, gather the yarn in the center, and stitch the yarn to the fabric so you have 6 inches on each side. This piece will hold the yarn down the center of the head.

3. Center the yarn just below the seam line on the top of the head so the yarn is on the forehead. Take small tacks along the part to attach the yarn to the top of the head. Cut a few strands in the front to create bangs.

4. Place a line of glue on each side of the head at the seam line to hold the yarn in place.

5. Cut the satin ribbon in half, gather the yarn in a bunch at each side, and tie.

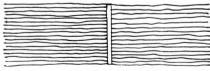

Figure 4

73

HER FIRST DOLLY ASSEMBLY PATTERNS

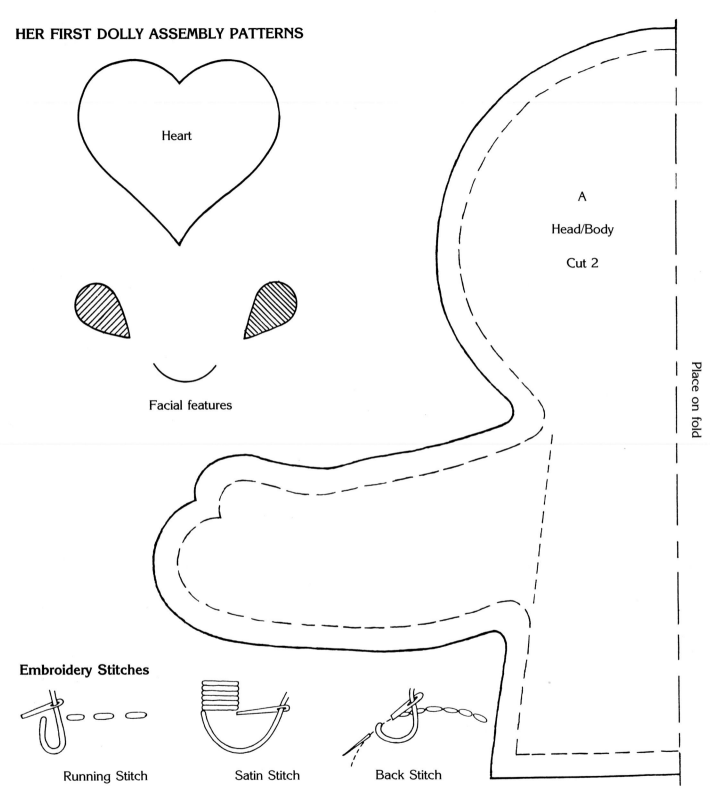

Heart

Facial features

A

Head/Body

Cut 2

Place on fold

Embroidery Stitches

Running Stitch

Satin Stitch

Back Stitch

74

HER FIRST DOLLY CLOTHES

Place on fold

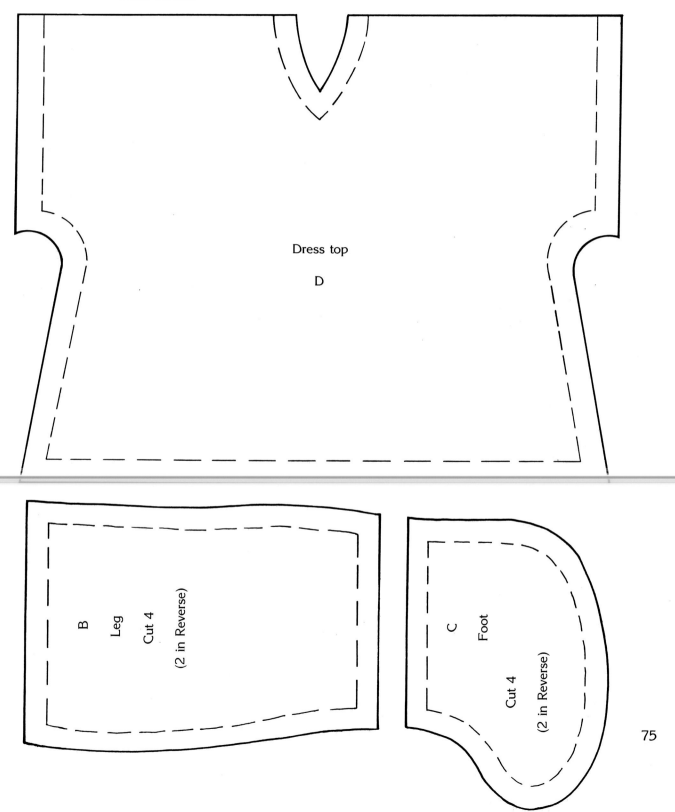

Dress top

D

B

Leg

Cut 4

(2 in Reverse)

C

Foot

Cut 4

(2 in Reverse)

75

Country Barnyard Quilt

Barnyard animals make delightful appliqués for a crib quilt. This quilt is 30 × 40 inches and was made with soft pastel calicos by Suzi Peterson. Each block contains a different animal. If you'd like to enlarge this project, add another fabric border all around the outside. Make it as wide as necessary. Or you can add two more borders to repeat the design as shown.

Materials

Note: All yardages are figured for 45-inch-wide fabric.

1½ yards peach print (borders and backing)
½ yard blue solid
¼ yard green print
¼ yard each of purple, blue, and light blue calicos
small piece (at least 7 × 7 inches) each of yellow, calico, peach calico, and
   2 different brown calicos
scraps of peach solid
1 yard quilt batting
1 skein each of black and blue embroidery floss
embroidery needle
tracing paper

Cutting List

Note: All measurements for the quilt include a ¼-inch seam allowance. The animal patterns are used full-size and do not need a seam allowance added when cutting as they will be machine-appliquéd with a zigzag stitch.

Trace animal patterns, feet, and tails and pin the tracings to the appropriate fabrics as indicated below.

For quilt cut the following:	For appliqués cut the following:
from peach print:	*from white solid:*
backing piece 30½ × 40½ inches	sheep body
2 strips, each 4½ × 40½ inches	bunny tail
(side borders)	*from black solid:*
2 strips, each 4½ × 22½ inches	sheep head
(top and bottom borders)	sheep feet
from blue solid:	*from blue solid:*
2 lattice strips, each 2½ × 32½ inches	bunny body
4 lattice strips, each 2½ × 18½ inches	*from yellow calico:*
3 lattice strips, each 2½ × 8½ inches	duck body
	hen beak
	hen feet
from green print:	*from peach calico:* cat
2 squares, each 8½ × 8½ inches	*from one brown calico:* dog
from purple calico:	*from other brown calico:*
2 squares, each 8½ × 8½ inches	hen body
from blue calico:	*from peach solid:*
1 square, 8½ × 8½ inches	duck bill
from light blue calico:	duck feet
1 square, 8½ × 8½ inches	hen head/neck

Directions

To appliqué blocks

1. Transfer the eyes and mouth from each pattern to the fabric animal face (see page 13).

2. Using 3 strands of black embroidery floss and a back stitch (see page 74), embroider the eyes and mouths.

3. Pin the cat to the center of a purple calico square, the duck to the center of the blue calico square, the bunny to the center of the light blue calico square, the dog to a green print square, the hen to the other green print square, and the sheep to the other purple calico square.

4. Set your sewing machine for a narrow zigzag stitch and, using thread to match each appliqué, stitch around each fabric piece.

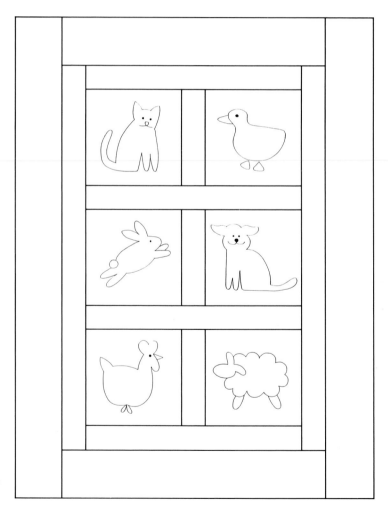

Country Barnyard Quilt
Assembly Diagram

To join blocks

1. With right sides facing, attach a 2½ × 8½-inch blue lattice strip to the right side of the cat block. Join this strip to the left side edge of the duck block to make the top row. Press seams to one side.

2. Repeat step 1 using the bunny block and the dog block separated by a 2½ × 8½-inch blue lattice strip for the middle row.

3. Repeat with the hen block and the sheep block for the bottom row. Press seams to one side.

To join rows

Refer to the assembly diagram.

1. With right sides facing, join a 2½ × 18½-inch lattice strip to the top edge of the top row. Next, stitch another lattice strip of the same size to the bottom edge of the top row. Press seams to one side.

2. Continue to join all 3 rows separated by 2½ × 18½-inch blue lattice strips in this way, ending with a blue lattice strip at the bottom of the pieced top. Press seams to one side.

3. With right sides facing, stitch the 2½ × 32½-inch blue lattice strips to each side of the quilt top. Press seams to one side.

To add borders

1. With right sides facing, stitch the 4½ × 22½-inch peach print strips to the top and bottom edges of the quilt top. Press seams to one side.

2. Next, join the two 4½ × 40½-inch peach print strips to the side edges in the same way. Press seams to one side.

To finish

1. Cut the quilt batting to the same size as the quilt top.

2. With right sides facing, pin the quilt top, backing, and then batting together.

3. Stitch around 3 sides and 4 corners, leaving the bottom edge open for turning.

4. Clip the corners and trim the seam allowance. Turn right side out.

5. Turn the raw edges of the top and backing to the inside ¼ inch and slip-stitch opening closed.

6. Using the blue embroidery floss, tie the quilt in each corner of each block and at each corner where the borders meet. To do this, cut an 8-inch length of embroidery floss. Thread the embroidery needle and insert it down through the top and up again so the ends are equal. Tie in a knot and clip the ends to within 1½ inches.

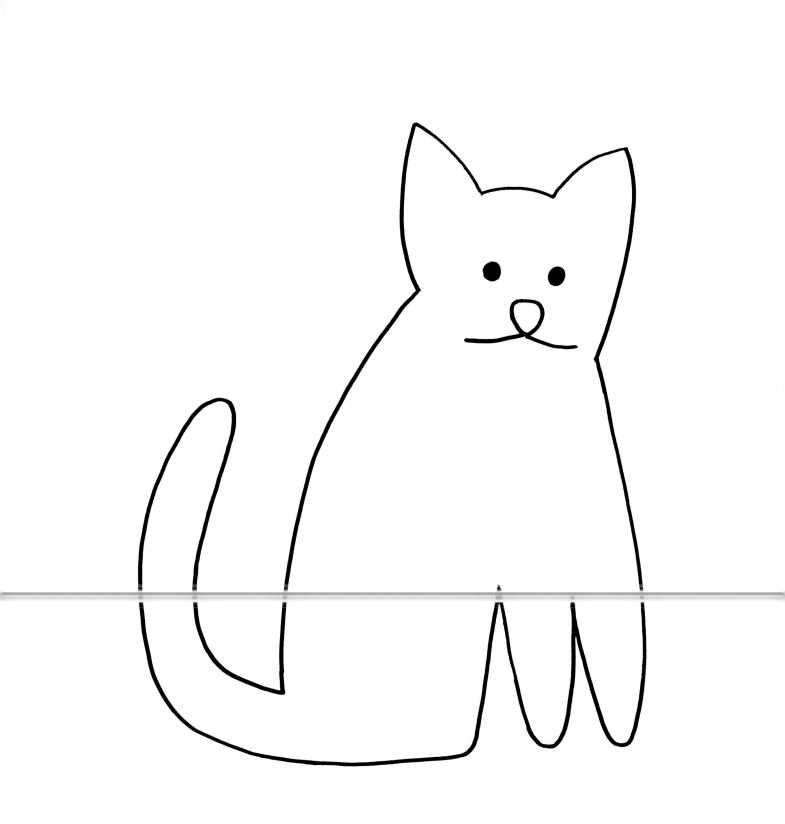

Toy Bags

Colorful striped fabric is used to make these bags for holding blocks, marbles, small toys, or jacks. Each bag is personalized with an appliqué name, and any child would love to have his or her very own. The bags were designed and made by Nancy Moore, of Orleans, Massachusetts, and the blocks were handmade by her husband, Bill, as Christmas presents for their grandchildren. The large bag is 12 inches high and the smaller one is 7 inches high.

Materials (for both bags)

Note: All yardages are figured for 45-inch-wide fabric. A heavyweight fabric, such as canvas, is recommended for its durability and will hold a shape better than a lightweight fabric.

> ½ yard white solid
> ¼ yard turquoise solid
> ¼ yard purple solid
> thread: turquoise and purple
> 1 yard ¼-inch cording for each bag

Cutting List

Note: All measurements include a ¼-inch seam allowance.

Trace and transfer circle patterns A and B for templates (see page 11).

For 12-inch bag cut the following:	*For 7-inch bag cut the following:*
from white solid:	*from white solid:*
9 strips, each 1½ × 9 inches	6 strips, each 1½ × 5 inches
1 piece 13½ × 18½ inches (for lining)	1 piece 8½ × 12½ inches (for lining)
1 circle from template A (for lining)	1 circle from template B (for lining)
1 name patch (see page 88)	1 name patch (see page 88)
from turquoise solid:	*from purple solid:*
9 strips, each 1½ × 9 inches	6 strips, each 1½ × 5 inches
1 piece 5½ × 18½ inches	1 strip 4½ × 12½ inches
1 circle from template A	1 circle from template B
letters for name (see page 89)	letters for name (see page 89)

Directions

To make 12-inch bag

1. With right sides facing, stitch a $1\frac{1}{2} \times 9$-inch turquoise strip to a $1\frac{1}{2} \times 9$-inch white strip along one long edge. Open seams and press.

2. Continue stitching the $1\frac{1}{2} \times 9$-inch strips together, alternating turquoise and white. This will give you a striped fabric piece 9 inches long and $18\frac{1}{2}$ inches wide.

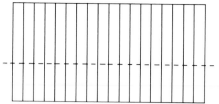

Figure 1

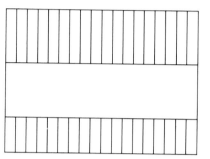

Figure 2

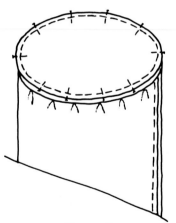

Figure 3

3. Refer to Figure 1. Measure 5½ inches down from the top and mark. Cut the fabric along this line. You will have 2 striped fabric pieces.

4. With right sides facing, stitch the top (5½ × 18½-inch) striped piece to the 5½ × 18½-inch solid turquoise piece along one long edge.

5. Refer to Figure 2. Stitch the bottom edge of the solid turquoise piece to the top edge of the striped bottom (3½ × 18½-inch) piece. Open seams and press.

To make appliqué name patch

1. Using the alphabet provided, trace the letters to be used from the book and transfer to cardboard for templates (see page 11).

2. Place each letter template on the back of the turquoise fabric and trace around the template. Cut out.

3. From the white fabric cut a piece 3½ inches by the length needed to fit the letters, plus ½ inch. For the bag shown with a four-letter name, we cut a piece 3½ × 6½ inches.

4. Pin the letters to the white fabric piece. Using matching thread and a zigzag stitch, sew around each letter.

5. Fold the raw edges of the appliquéd patch under ¼ inch on each side and press. Center and pin this to the green midsection of the bag.

6. Stitch around each side as close to the edge as possible.

To finish

1. With right sides facing, fold the bag in half. Starting 1½ inches from the top, stitch down the side to make a tube.

2. Refer to Figure 3. Next, with right sides facing, pin the turquoise bottom circle A to the bottom opening of the bag, taking small tucks in the bag as you work the fabric around the circle.

3. Stitch around. Turn right side out.

4. With right sides facing, fold the 13½ × 18½-inch white lining piece in half. Starting 1½ inches from the top, stitch down one side to make a tube. Pin the bottom lining circle A to the bag and stitch as in step 2.

5. Insert the lining inside the bag. Trim the top edges of the bag and lining so they are even.

6. Fold the top edge over to the inside ¼ inch and press. Place the cording on the top edge of the fabric and fold over again 1 inch, encasing the cording inside the fold. Stitch all around.

To make 7-inch bag

This bag is made in the same way as the 12-inch bag *except:* In step 3 (this page and Figure 1), after stitching the strips together, measure 3½ inches from the top rather than 5½ inches, mark, and cut.

Since the 7-inch bag is smaller around, you might want to use initials unless the name has only 3 or 4 letters.

88

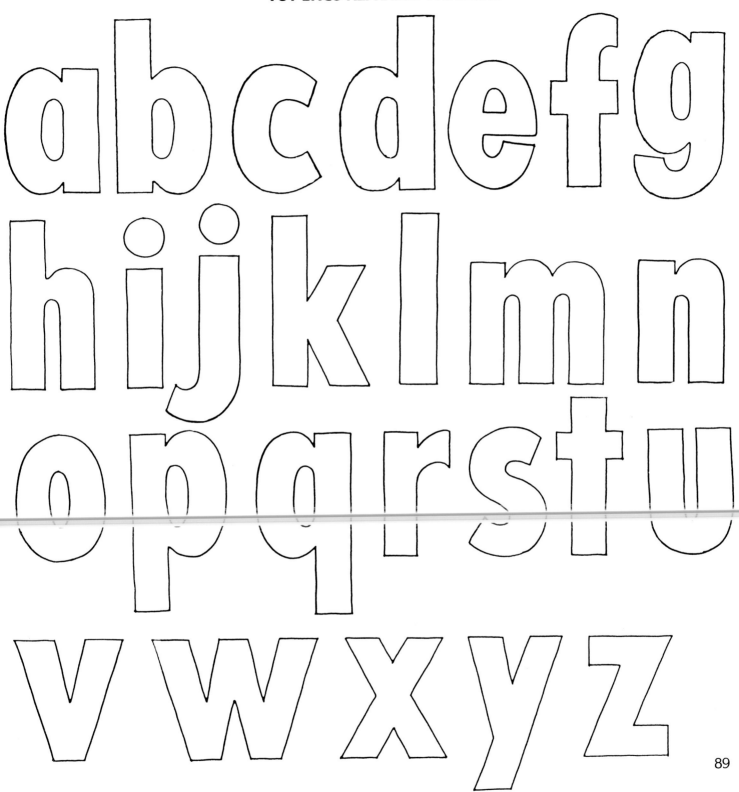

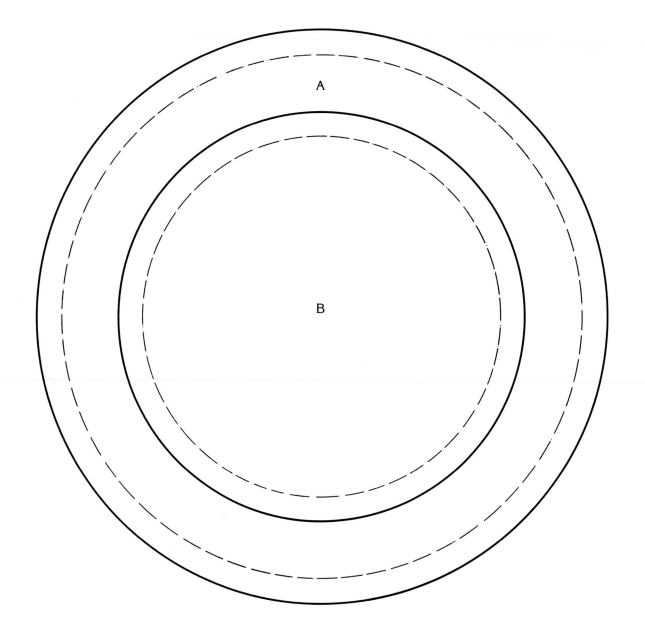

A

B

Duffel Bag

A duffel bag is handy for carrying baby items, overnight necessities, gym equipment, etc. It's not easy to find pretty as well as serviceable bags to purchase. This one, designed by Nancy Moore, combines a pretty paisley print with solid colors of green and burgundy set off by strips of black. The black straps are made of heavy canvas and the lining is made of muslin. A nice detail on each end is the piping made from the paisley fabric. The finished size is an ample 24 inches long by 11½ inches high.

Materials

Note: All yardages are figured for 45-inch-wide fabric.

⅓ yard burgundy solid
½ yard paisley print
¼ yard black solid
¼ yard green solid
1½ yards lining fabric
42 inches 1-inch-wide black canvas strap
20-inch black zipper
2½ yards ¼-inch cording
tracing paper

Cutting List

Note: All measurements include a ¼-inch seam allowance unless stated otherwise.

The pattern shown on page 94 is only ¼ of the end circle. Trace this pattern, then turn the tracing and line up the dotted lines to trace again for the second half of the circle. Repeat to make a full-circle pattern.

Cut the following:

from burgundy solid:
    2 strips, each 3½ × 36½ inches
    2 circles

from paisley print:
    2 strips, each 5½ × 36½ inches
    2 strips, each 1½ × 38 inches
      (piping)

from black solid:
    4 strips, each 1½ × 36½ inches

from green solid:
    1 strip 4½ × 36½ inches

from lining fabric:
    1 piece 24½ × 36½ inches
    2 circles

Directions

To make pieced top Refer to Figure 1.

1. With right sides facing, stitch a 3½×36½-inch burgundy strip to a 1½×36½-inch black strip along one long edge. Press seams to one side.
2. Next, stitch a 5½×36½-inch paisley strip to the opposite side of the black strip.
3. Continue in this way, with another 1½-inch-wide black strip, followed by the 4½×36½-inch green strip, then another black strip, the other 5½-inch-wide paisley strip, followed by another black strip, and end with the other 3½-inch-wide burgundy strip. Press seams to one side.

Lining

1. Cut the lining piece the same size as the pieced top.
2. With wrong sides facing, pin the lining and top pieces together.
3. Working from the front of the fabric, stitch along each seam line to join top and lining pieces.
4. With wrong sides facing and using a ⅛-inch seam allowance, stitch the lining circles to the burgundy circles all around.

To make piping

1. Cut cording in half and place each piece on the wrong side of each 1½×38-inch paisley strip.
2. Fold the fabric over the cording, matching long raw edges so the cording is encased in the fabric.
3. Using the zipper foot on your sewing machine, stitch as close to the cording as possible.
4. With raw edges aligned, pin the piping to the right side of each circle piece. Clip into the seam allowance as you turn and pin the piping around the fabric. Overlap the piping ends.
5. Use the piping stitches as a guide and stitch all around.

To assemble bag

1. With right sides facing and raw edges aligned, fold the bag piece in half horizontally.
2. Locate the top edge of the bag and stitch 2 inches in from each side.
3. Insert the zipper according to package directions.
4. With right sides facing and piping between, pin each end piece in place all around.
5. Stitch around each end to attach the circles, as shown in Figure 2.
6. Open the zipper and turn the bag right side out.

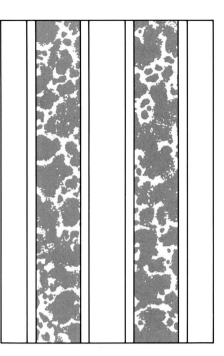

Figure 1

Figure 2

93

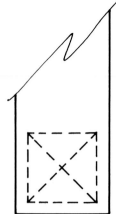

Figure 3

To add handles

1. Cut the 42-inch black canvas strap in half and fold each raw end of each strap under 1½ inches.

2. To create a handle, pin each folded end of one strap to the outside of the bag approximately 1¼ inches down from the zipper on the center black strips on one side of the bag. Repeat on the other side of the bag.

3. Stitch the folded ends of the straps to the fabric (see Figure 3).

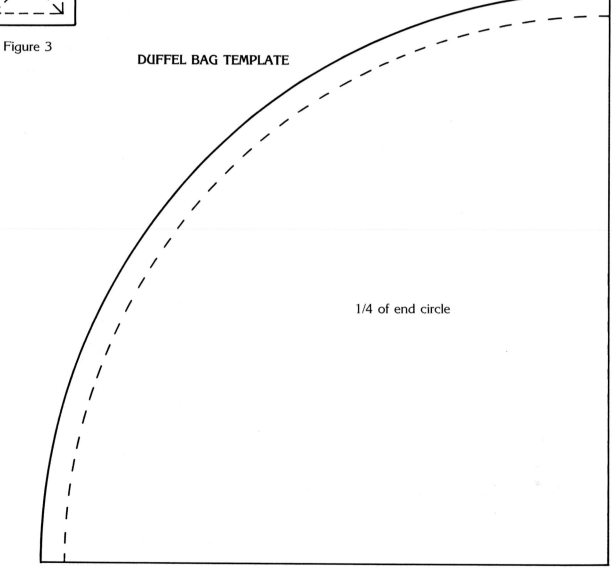

DUFFEL BAG TEMPLATE

1/4 of end circle

Jewelry Bag

Whenever you're working on a project there's bound to be leftover fabric that goes into the scrap basket. I always try to include projects for using up scraps, but sometimes it's nice to make something small to match the item from which the scraps came. This little bag for jewelry or small items matches the Duffel Bag project on page 91 and is 4½ × 6 inches.

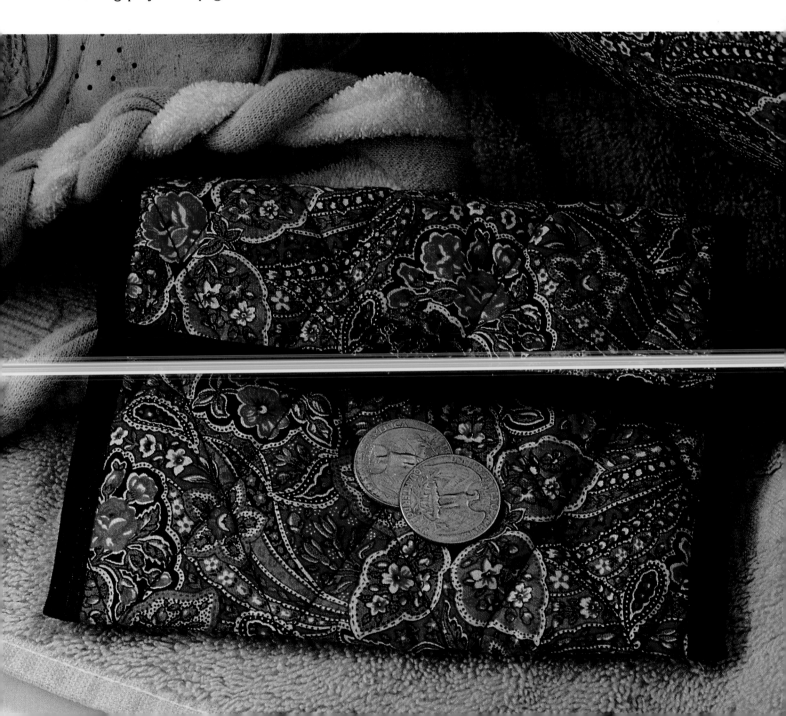

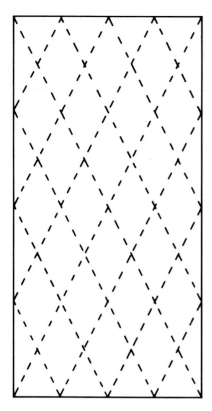

Figure 1

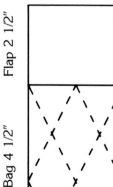

Figure 2

Materials

small piece each of paisley print and burgundy solids
quilt batting $6 \times 11\frac{1}{2}$ inches
1 yard double-fold ¼-inch seam binding
1 large button or snap

Cutting List

Note: All measurements include ¼-inch seam allowance.

> ### Cut the following:
>
> *from paisley print:*
>   1 piece $6\frac{1}{2} \times 12$ inches
>
> *from burgundy solid:*
>   1 piece $6\frac{1}{2} \times 12$ inches (lining)

Directions

To quilt

1. On the right side of the paisley piece, draw a grid of $1\frac{1}{4}$-inch diagonal lines in both directions, as shown in Figure 1.
2. With wrong sides facing and batting between, pin the paisley and lining pieces together.
3. Machine-quilt on all marked lines (see page 14).

To finish

1. With right sides facing, pin the seam binding over the raw edges all around.
2. (See Figure 2.) With the lining on the inside, fold one short end of the quilted piece over 4½ inches and pin the side edges together. Stitch.
3. Make the buttonhole in the center of the top flap and add a corresponding button on the pouch. Or sew on a snap to close the bag.

Pinwheel Carry-All

Everyone needs a sturdy canvas tote. This one was designed by Nancy Moore, who custom-designs and makes products for boats and boaters. She made this carry-all with two beautifully detailed outside pockets and a nice, wide shoulder strap. The bag is lined with bright blue and the straps are lined with the fabric used for the pinwheel designs. The carry-all measures 10 × 14 inches.

Materials

Note: All yardages are figured for 45-inch-wide fabric.

　　1 yard off-white canvas
　　¼ yard pastel floral print
　　1 yard bright blue solid (lining)
　　tracing paper
　　cardboard

Cutting List

Note: All measurements include a ¼-inch seam allowance.

Trace patterns A and B and transfer to cardboard for templates (see page 11). Enlarge and trace end piece pattern C (see page 11).

Cut the following:	*from pastel floral print:*
from off-white canvas:	13 - A
8 - A	1 piece 2½ × 34½ inches (strap lining)
2 - B	
2 - C	*from bright blue solid:*
1 piece 15 × 34½ inches	2 - C (lining for end pieces)
1 piece 2½ × 34½ inches (strap)	1 piece 15 × 34½ inches (bag lining)

Directions

To make pinwheel pockets

Each pocket uses 4 calico A pieces, 4 canvas A pieces, and 1 canvas B piece.

1. Refer to Figures 1-3. With wrong sides facing, fold all 13 floral print A pieces in half diagonally and press. Fold again into smaller triangles. (Save 5 folded triangles for the flap edge.) All the raw edges should be lined up evenly. The triangles will have one side with a double-folded edge and one side with 2

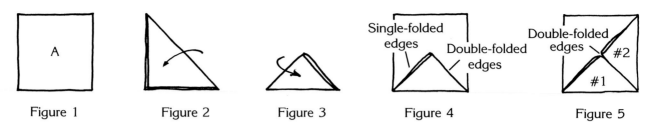

Figure 1   Figure 2   Figure 3   Figure 4   Figure 5

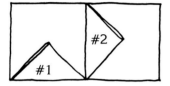

Figure 6

Open and press

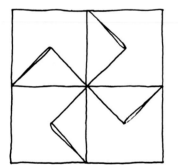

Figure 7

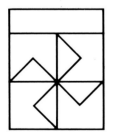

Figure 8

Figure 9

single-folded edges. These edges will be referred to for correct placement on the background squares and the border of the bag flap.

2. With right sides facing and raw edges aligned, pin 1 triangle to one side edge of a canvas A square as shown in Figure 4. Make 4 in this way.

3. Refer to Figure 5 and pin a second triangle next to the first triangle so that the double-folded edges fit together tightly.

4. Pin another canvas A square over the pinned triangle section and stitch along one side edge only, as shown in Figure 6. Open the squares and press the second triangle toward the second square as shown in Figure 7. Repeat with the remaining canvas A squares and floral print triangles.

5. Refer to Figure 8 for placement. With right sides facing and 4 triangle points in the center, pin 2 sets together and stitch along one long edge. Open and press.

6. With right sides facing, stitch the long edge of a B piece to the top edge of each pinwheel block as shown in Figure 9. Press seams to one side.

7. Then fold the top edge of each pocket under ¼ inch and, with your machine set for a long stitch, sew across. Fold the bottom and side edges under ¼ inch and press.

To line pieces

1. Turn the raw edges of the canvas bag piece to the inside ¼ inch and press.

2. Repeat with the 2 canvas C pieces, the 2½ × 34½-inch canvas strap, and all lining pieces.

3. With wrong sides facing, pin the canvas C pieces to the blue C pieces and stitch all around.

4. Repeat with the canvas strap and the floral print strap lining.

5. Refer to Figure 10. With wrong sides facing, pin the 15 × 34½-inch canvas bag piece to the same-size blue lining piece. Pin the long raw edges of the remaining 5 folded floral print triangles between the canvas and the lining across the short top edge. Stitch all around.

Figure 10

To assemble bag

1. With right sides facing, start at the bottom corner of the side of the bag piece and pin to the top (short end) corner of a C end piece. Pin down one side of the C piece, across the bottom edge, and up the other side, as shown in Figure 11. The remainder of the bag piece is the flap.

2. Stitch down the side, across the bottom, and up the other side of the C piece. Repeat with the other C piece.

3. Pin the short ends of the strap to the end of the inside top edge of the bag. Stitch across (see the assembly diagram).

To add pockets

1. Pin the pocket pieces to the front flap so that one side and bottom edges align with the edges of the flap.

2. Using the stitch lines as a guide, sew down each side and across the bottom of each pocket to finish the bag.

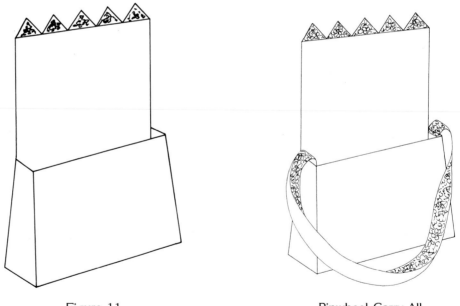

Figure 11

Pinwheel Carry-All
Assembly Diagram

PINWHEEL CARRY-ALL TEMPLATES

PINWHEEL CARRY-ALL PATTERN

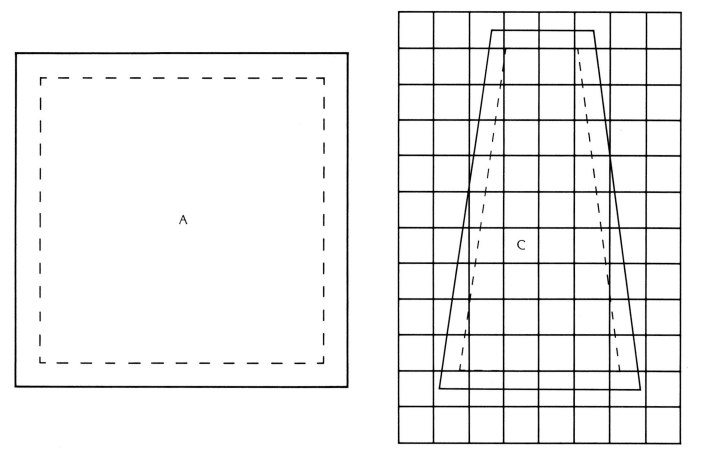

Each square equals 1 inch

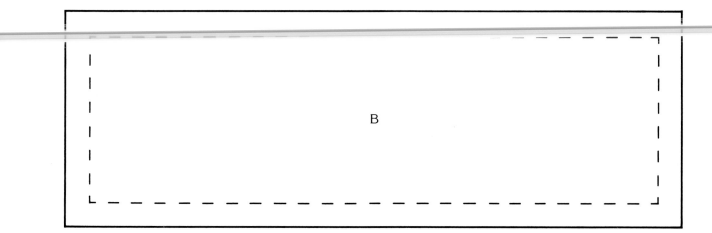

Pinwheel Pillows

If you have leftover canvas and floral print fabric from the Pinwheel Carry-All (page 97), you might like to use it to make little sachets or throw pillows. Once you know how easy it is to create the pattern, it's fun to use this skill for making small gifts or items to sell at bazaars. The pillows are 6 × 6 inches and can be filled with pine needles or potpourri.

Materials (for 2 pillows)

Note: All yardages are figured for 45-inch-wide fabric.

> ¼ yard muslin
> ⅛ yard pastel floral print
> 25 inches of ruffle or lace for each pillow
> stuffing
> tracing paper
> cardboard

Cutting List

Note: All measurements include a ¼-inch seam allowance.

Trace pattern A (page 101); transfer to cardboard for template (see page 11).

Cut the following:

from muslin:
> 8 - A (4 for each pillow)
> 2 pieces, each 6½ × 6½ inches
> (1 for each pillow)

from pastel floral print:
> 8 - A (4 for each pillow)

Directions

Follow steps 1 through 4 from the Pinwheel Carry-All on page 97. This is the pillow top.

To finish

1. With right sides facing and raw edges aligned, pin the ruffle or lace around the pillow top. Overlap the ends. Stitch around.
2. With right sides facing, pin a 6½ × 6½-inch muslin piece to the pillow top with the ruffle or lace between.
3. Stitch around 3 sides and 4 corners. Clip the corners and turn right side out. Press.
4. Stuff each pillow. Turn raw edges to the inside and slip-stitch closed.

Take-Along Quilt

A take-along quilt is perfect for sleepovers because it folds up neatly to fit into its own attached pouch. Karen Schwenk made two take-along quilts for her nieces. The photograph shows one quilt and the pouch of the other. The quilt is 44¾ × 62¼ inches and the pocket pouch is 18 inches square. Materials and instructions follow for the quilt shown and its matching pouch. (If you prefer the design shown in the pouch, the information given will help you determine the yardages required.)

Materials

Note: All yardages are figured for 45-inch-wide fabric.

- 1¾ yards backing fabric
- 1¼ yards pink paisley or calico
- 1¼ yards blue calico
- 1 yard pink solid
- 1 yard blue print
- ¼ yard pink pin dot or small print (for binding)
- 2¼ yards quilt batting
- package ⅛-inch-wide satin ribbon for tying

Cutting List

Note: All measurements include a ¼-inch seam allowance.

Cut the following:

from backing fabric:
   1 piece 45 × 63¼ inches

from pink paisley or calico:
   18 strips, each 2¼ × 37 inches (for quilt)
   12 strips, each 1½ × 16½ inches (for pouch)

from blue calico:
   18 strips, each 2¼ × 37 inches (for quilt)
   12 strips, each 1½ × 16½ inches (for pouch)

from pink solid:
   9 strips, each 2¼ × 37 inches (for quilt)

   6 strips, each 1½ × 16½ inches (for pouch)

from blue print:
   4 strips, each 2 × 15½ inches (pouch top and bottom borders)
   4 strips, each 2 × 18½ inches (pouch side borders)
   2 pieces, each 18½ × 18½ inches (pouch lining)

from pink pin dot or small print:
   5 strips cut on the bias, each 1½ × 45 inches

103

Directions

Quilt

To make blocks

See the instructions for strip piecing on page 16. Refer to Figure 1.

1. With right sides facing, stitch a 2¼ × 37-inch pink paisley or calico strip to a same-size blue calico strip along one long edge.
2. Next, stitch this to a 2¼ × 37-inch pink solid strip in the same way, followed by another blue calico strip, then another pink paisley or calico strip. Press seams to one side. Make 9 sets in this way.
3. Measure and cut each set into 9¼-inch blocks. You will have 36 blocks, but will only use 35.

Figure 1

To make rows

1. Refer to Figure 2. Arrange 5 blocks in a row.
2. With right sides facing, stitch the right side of the first block to the left side of the second block. Continue to join all 5 blocks in this way to make a row. Press seams to one side. Make 4 rows in this way.
3. Refer to Figure 3 and arrange 5 blocks in a row. To make a row, stitch all 5 blocks together as you did in step 2. Press seams to one side. Make 3 rows in this way.

Figure 2

To join rows

Refer to the assembly diagram.

1. With right sides facing, stitch the bottom edge of the first row (Figure 2) to the top edge of the second row (Figure 3). Press seams to one side.
2. Continue to join all 7 rows in this way, alternating them as you do so. Press seams to one side.

Figure 3

To tie

1. With wrong sides facing, pin the pieced top, batting, and backing together.
2. Starting at the center of the quilt and working outward in a sunburst pattern, take long, loose basting stitches through all 3 layers (see page 14).
3. Make small bows with the satin ribbon and stitch through all layers at the corners and center of each block to secure.
4. Trim the batting and backing to the same size as the quilt top.

To finish

1. With right sides facing, stitch the five 1½ × 45-inch pin dot bias strips together at the short ends to make one strip at least 6 yards long.
2. With wrong sides facing, fold the strip in half lengthwise and press. Open the strip. You will have a crease line down the center.
3. Fold each long edge into the center line and press. Fold in half lengthwise again.

Take-Along Quilt Assembly Diagram

4. Pin the seam binding along each edge of the quilt so the raw edges are inside the fold of the seam binding. When you reach the end, turn the raw edge under ½ inch and overlap the other end to finish.

5. Slip-stitch the binding to the quilt top along the sides and bottom edges only. Leave the top edge pinned for now and do not stitch at this time.

Pouch

To make blocks

Refer to the strip-piecing instructions on page 16.

1. Using the 1½ × 16½-inch strips, repeat quilt steps 1 and 2 on page 105. Make 6 sets in this way.

2. Measure and cut each set into 5½-inch blocks. There will be 18 blocks.

To join blocks

1. Refer to Figure 4. Arrange 9 of the blocks into 3 rows of 3 blocks each as shown.

2. With right sides facing, stitch 3 blocks together to make a row. Make all 3 rows in this way. Press seams to one side.

3. With right sides facing, stitch all 3 rows together. Press seams to one side.

4. See Figure 5. With right sides facing, stitch 2 × 15½-inch blue print strips to the top and bottom edges. Next, stitch a 2 × 18½-inch blue print strip to each side. Press seams to one side.

5. Repeat steps 1 through 4 for the back of the pouch.

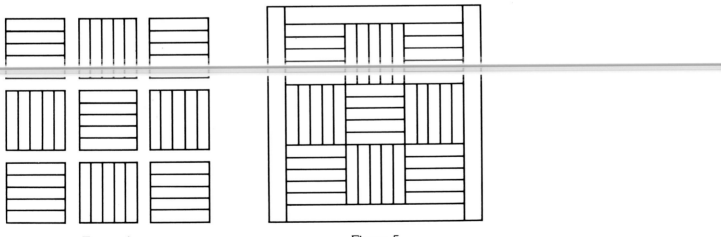

Figure 4   Figure 5

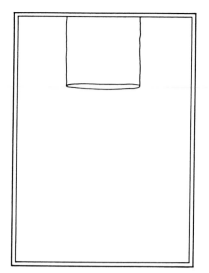

Figure 6

To quilt

1. Cut 2 pieces of batting the same size as the pouch top.
2. Pin the pieced top to one piece of quilt batting and take small running stitches on each side of all seams.
3. Repeat for the back piece.

To assemble

1. With right sides facing, stitch the front and back quilted pieces together along each side, leaving the top and bottom edges open.
2. With right sides facing, stitch the 2 blue print lining pieces (18½ × 18½ inches) together along each side in the same way. Turn the lining right side out.
3. With right sides facing and side seams matching, slip the lining inside the outer pouch.
4. Stitch the top edge of the lining and the outside piece together. Pull the lining out (remember: the bottom edge hasn't been stitched, so you can do this) and fold the top edge down over the batting. The lining is now on the outside with the quilted front and back pieces on the inside. The bottom edge is still unstitched.
5. Find the center of the top edge of the quilt and tuck the bottom raw edges of the pouch under the seam binding on the quilt as shown in Figure 6. Pin in place.
6. Stitch the seam binding to the quilt top along the top edge, enclosing the bottom edge of the pouch between the seam binding and the quilt top as you do so.

To fold

1. From the quilt back, fold the side edges to meet in the center.
2. Start at the bottom and fold the quilt to the pouch.
3. Turn the pouch right side out over the folded quilt. It will all tuck neatly inside.

Scrap Pillow

Once you've made one of these little pillows, you'll want to make a bunch. They're so easy and it's always fun to make something from scraps. I often find that the most interesting projects evolve from playing around with bits of fabric. Almost any way you arrange them will look good. In our first annual quilting book for the Better Homes and Gardens® Crafts Club, *Country Patchwork & Quilting*, we offered an antique quilt made from scraps. It was extremely popular and I received many letters from readers who enjoyed making it.

This pillow is 12 × 12 inches and has no piping or ruffles. It's a basic country-style patchwork project, simple and direct.

Materials

scraps of various calicos
backing piece 12½ × 12½ inches
stuffing or a 12-inch pillow form
thin quilt batting 12 × 12 inches
tracing paper
cardboard

Cutting List

Note: All measurements include a ¼-inch seam allowance.

Trace patterns A and B and transfer to cardboard for templates (see page 11). Place templates on wrong side of the fabric and trace around each one.

Figure 1

Cut the following:

from calicos:
4 - A
28 - B

Directions

To make squares

With right sides facing, stitch 2 different color B pieces together along the diagonal to make a square (Figure 1). Press seams to one side. Make 8.

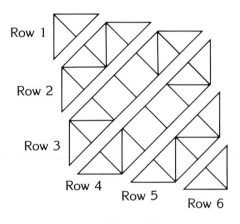

Figure 2

To assemble

1. Arrange the squares and the 12 remaining B triangles into rows according to Figure 2.
2. With right sides facing, stitch the short edge of a B piece to another B piece to make a larger triangle for the first row. Press seams to one side.
3. Continue to join the pieces in each row as shown in Figure 2.
4. With right sides facing, join Rows 1 and 2. Press seams to one side.
5. Continue to join all 6 rows in this way, as shown in the assembly diagram.

To quilt

1. Pin the patchwork top to the thin quilt batting.
2. Using small running stitches, quilt ¼ inch on each side of all seam lines.

To finish

1. With right sides facing, pin the quilted top to the backing fabric.
2. Stitch around 3 sides and 4 corners, leaving one side open for turning.
3. Clip corners and trim seam allowance. Turn right side out and press.
4. Stuff loosely with stuffing or use a 12-inch pillow form. Turn the raw edges of the back and front pieces to the inside and slip-stitch closed.

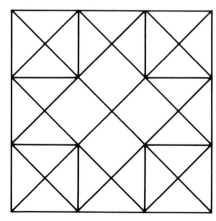

Scrap Pillow Assembly Diagram

SCRAP PILLOW TEMPLATES

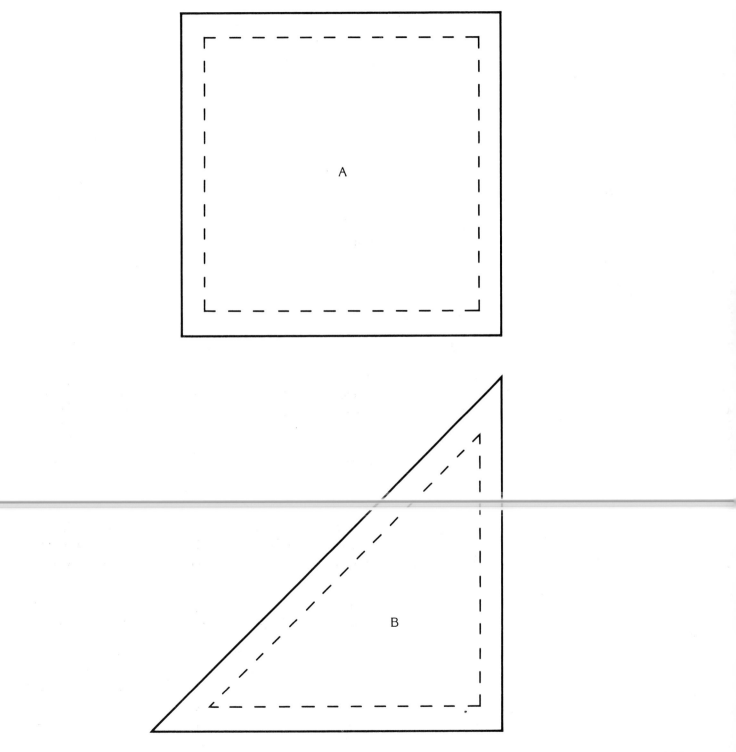

Miniature Log Cabin Wall Hanging

This 11½ × 15¼-inch wall hanging is perfect for decorating a niche or narrow area. The soft colors make it just right for a bedroom. Karen Schwenk used scraps of pastel prints and solids to create this little beauty. It's easy to hang on the wall with Velcro® tabs.

Materials

Note: All yardages are figured for 45-inch-wide fabric.

> ¼ yard pale blue gingham
> pink backing piece 12¼ × 16 inches
> light blue calico strip, 4 × 12 inches (inner border)
> small pieces of different light and dark calicos
> quilt batting
> 1 skein pink embroidery floss
> embroidery needle
> small piece ⅛-inch satin ribbon (optional)
> Velcro® tabs for hanging

Cutting List

Note: Because the pieces are so narrow, all measurements include only a ⅛-inch seam allowance rather than the usual ¼-inch allowance.

Tip: The Log Cabin pattern is made from strips of fabric that are cut into the right-size units as you build the block from a center square. The length of the strips you use should be comfortable to work with. Since this project is small and no single unit in a block is longer than 2 inches, you might cut your strips into 12-inch-long pieces for easy handling.

Cut the following:

from pale blue gingham:
2 strips, each 1¾ × 12¾ inches (outer side borders)
2 strips, each 1¾ × 11½ inches (outer top and bottom borders)

from light blue calico strip:
2 strips, each ⅝ × 11¾ (inner side borders)

2 strips, each ⅝ × 8¾ inches (inner top and bottom borders)

from light calicos:
48 squares, each ⅝ × ⅝ inches from remaining fabric cut ⅝ × 12-inch-long strips

from dark calicos:
⅝ × 12-inch-long strips

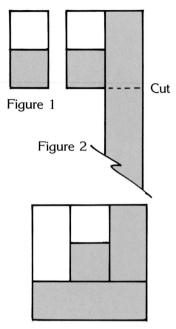

Figure 1

Figure 2

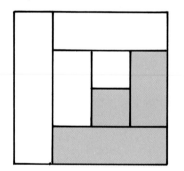

Figure 3

Cut

Figure 4

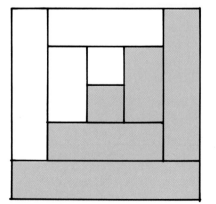

Figure 5

Directions

To make a block

1. With right sides facing, join 2 light calico squares along one edge, as shown in Figure 1. Press seams to one side.

2. With right sides facing, join a dark strip along one side edge as shown in Figure 2. Cut excess fabric. Press seams to dark side. Repeat with a light strip to the outer side edge of this unit (see Figure 3).

3. With right sides facing, join a dark strip to the bottom edge of the unit as shown in Figure 3. Repeat with a light strip on the top edge of the unit (see Figure 4).

4. With right sides facing, join a light strip to the left side edge of the unit as shown in Figure 4. Repeat with a dark strip on the right side edge of the unit (see Figure 5). Press seams to the dark side.

5. Continue by adding a dark strip to the bottom edge of the unit to complete the block as shown in Figure 5. Make 12 of these blocks.

6. Using different light and dark calicos, make 12 more blocks in the same way.

To make a row

Refer to the assembly diagram.

1. With right sides facing and dark half of each block matching, stitch along the right side edge. Open and press seams to one side.

2. With right sides facing and light half of each block matching, join the next block in the same way.

3. Next, match the dark half of the blocks and join the last block to complete the row of 4 blocks. Press seams to the dark side.

4. Refer to the assembly diagram and make 6 rows.

To join rows

1. With right sides facing, stitch Row 1 and Row 2 together. Open and press seams to one side.

2. Continue to join each row in this way.

To add borders

1. With right sides facing, pin the ⅝ × 11¾-inch light blue calico border strips to each side edge of the quilt top. Stitch together. Press seams to one side.

2. Repeat with the ⅝ × 8¾-inch light blue calico strips at the top and bottom edges of the quilt.

3. With right sides facing and raw edges aligned, join the 1¾ × 12¾-inch pale blue gingham strips to each side edge of the quilt top. Press seams to one side.

4. Repeat with the 1¾ × 12¾-inch pale blue gingham strips at the top and bottom edges of the quilt top.

To tie

1. With wrong sides facing, pin the quilt top, batting, and backing together. The backing will be slightly larger all around.

2. Insert the embroidery needle threaded with floss through all 3 layers of fabric in the center of each block. Bring up from the back as close as possible to where you inserted the needle and tie. Repeat. Cut the floss to ¾ inch. Repeat at each corner of each block.

3. Find the center of the quilt and tack a small ribbon bow if desired.

To finish

1. Trim the batting to same size as quilt top.

2. Turn the excess backing edges forward ¼ inch and press. Fold again over the edge of the quilt top all around and pin in place.

3. Slip-stitch all around to finish.

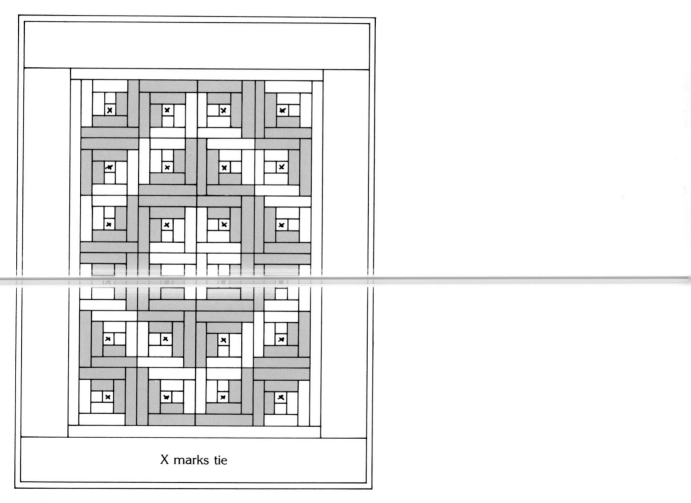

X marks tie

Miniature Log Cabin Wall Hanging Assembly Diagram

HOME FOR THE HOLIDAYS

Mini Log Cabin Pillows

The Log Cabin pattern is always attractive and easily adaptable for a project of any size. We've used this popular pattern to make small pillows with a red and white theme, as was often the choice of early quilters. You can fill the 8 × 8-inch pillows with stuffing or with pine needles to add a fresh scent to a room. The hand-quilting gives them a special, old-fashioned look.

Materials

Note: All yardages are figured for 45-inch-wide fabric.

¼ yard red solid
¼ yard white solid
1 yard premade piping for each pillow
stuffing
quilt batting

Cutting List (for 3 pillows)

Note: All measurements include a ¼-inch seam allowance.

Cut the following:

from red solid:
2 backing pieces, each 8½ × 8½ inches
1 square 2½ × 2½ inches
1 square 1½ × 1½ inches
from remaining fabric cut 1½-inch-wide strips

from white solid:
1 backing piece 8½ × 8½ inches
1 square 2½ × 2½ inches
1 square 1½ × 1½ inches
from remaining fabric cut 1½-inch-wide strips

Directions

Pillow 1

1. With right sides facing, stitch a red strip to one side of the 2½ × 2½-inch white square, as shown in Figure 1. Cut off the remainder of the red strip. Press seams to one side.

2. Next, stitch the red strip to the opposite side of the white square. Cut off the remainder of the strip, as shown in Figure 2. Press seams to one side.

3. (See Figure 3.) With right sides facing, join a white strip to the top edge of this unit. Cut off the remainder of the white strip and stitch it to the bottom edge of this unit.

4. Continue adding a red strip to each side and a white strip to the top and bottom edges 2 more times, as shown in Figure 4. Press seams to one side.

Pillow 2

1. With right sides facing, stitch a white strip to the top edge of the red 2½ × 2½-inch square, as shown in Figure 5. Cut off the remainder of the white strip. Press seams to one side.

2. Next, stitch the white strip to the right side of the red square, as shown in Figure 6. Cut off the remainder of the strip. Press seams to one side.

3. With right sides facing, stitch a red strip to the bottom edge of this unit. Cut off the remainder of the red strip and stitch this to the left side of the unit, as shown in Figure 7. Press seams to one side.

4. Attach a white strip to the top and one to the right side of the unit, then a red strip to the bottom and another to the left side of the unit 2 more times, as shown in Figure 8. Press seams to one side.

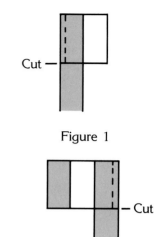

Figure 1

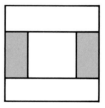

Figure 2

Figure 3

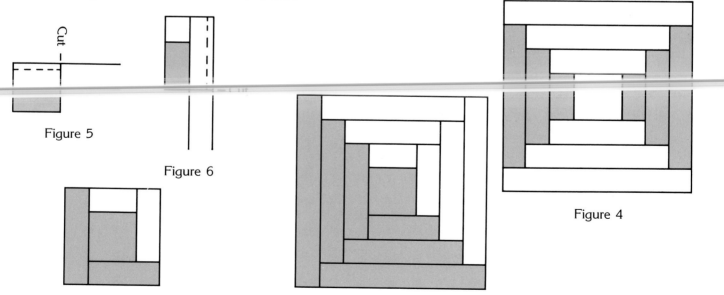

Figure 5

Figure 6

Figure 7

Figure 8

Figure 4

Pillow 3

1. With right sides facing, stitch the white $1\frac{1}{2} \times 1\frac{1}{2}$-inch square to the red $1\frac{1}{2} \times 1\frac{1}{2}$-inch square along one side edge, as shown in Figure 9.

2. Next, stitch a red strip to the top edge of this unit, as shown in Figure 10. Cut off the remainder of the red strip. Press seams to one side.

3. With right sides facing, stitch a white strip to the left side of this unit. Cut off the remainder of the white strip and stitch to the bottom edge of the unit, as shown in Figure 11. Press seams to one side.

4. Next, stitch a red strip to the right side of the unit. Cut off the remainder of the strip and join to the top of the unit, as shown in Figure 12.

5. Join a white strip to the left side and another white strip to the bottom edge of the unit, then a red strip to the right side and another to the top edge 2 more times, as shown in Figure 13. Press seams to one side.

Note: To make these pillows larger, continue the pattern by adding strips to each side in the same way.

To quilt

1. Pin each pillow top to a piece of batting slightly larger than the top.

2. Using small running stitches, quilt $\frac{1}{8}$ inch on each side of all seam lines.

Tip: Most quilting stitches on large projects are $\frac{1}{4}$ inch on each side of the seam lines, but when your strips are quite narrow and the project is small, the quilting looks better closer to the seam lines.

To finish

1. When all quilting has been completed, remove the pins and trim the batting $\frac{1}{2}$ inch smaller than the pillow tops all around.

2. With right sides facing, pin the piping to the pillow tops, overlapping where the ends meet.

3. Using the zipper foot on your sewing machine, stitch close to the piping all around (see page 16).

4. With right sides facing, pin a backing piece to each pillow top. Using the piping stitches as a guide, stitch around 3 sides and 4 corners.

5. Clip the corners, turn right side out, and stuff. Turn the raw edges of the opening to the inside and slip-stitch closed.

Figure 9

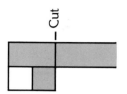

Figure 10

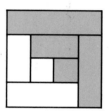

Figure 11

Figure 12

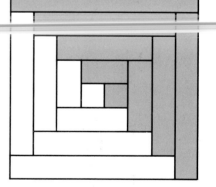

Figure 13

119

Country Tree Skirt

Dress up your holidays with a tree skirt. This is the time to use all the wonderful Christmas prints of red and green available in the fabric shops. Nancy Moore designed this project with a variety of traditional patchwork squares. The finished size is 58 inches around.

Materials

Note: All yardages are figured for 45-inch-wide fabric.

- 1 yard green solid (for tree skirt)
- ¼ yard red solid
- ¼ yard green solid
- ¼ yard each of 3 different green calicos (light and darker shades)
- ¼ yard each of 5 different red calicos (light and darker shades)
- 8 yards ½-inch double-fold green seam binding
- tracing paper
- cardboard

Cutting List

Note: All measurements include a ¼-inch seam allowance.

Enlarge and trace the diamond pattern (see page 11). Trace patterns A, B, C, D, and E and transfer each to cardboard for templates (see page 11).

Cut the following:

from green solid:
  8 diamond pieces

For Block 1 (Log Cabin) cut the following:

from red solid:
  1 - A

from light green calico:
  1 strip 2½ × 4½ inches (A)

from dark green calico:
  1 strip 2½ × 6½ inches (B)

from red calico 1:
  1 strip 2½ × 6½ inches (C)

from red calico 2:
  1 strip 2½ × 8½ inches (D)

from green solid:
  1 strip 2½ × 8½ inches (E)

from green calico:
  1 strip 2½ × 10½ inches (F)

from dark red calico 1:
  1 strip 2½ × 10½ inches (G)

from dark red calico 2:
  1 strip 2½ × 12½ inches (H)

For Block 2 (Basket) cut the following:

from light green calico:
  5 - B
  1 - C
  7 - D

from dark green calico:
  1 - C
  7 - D

For Block 3 (Pinwheel) cut the following:

from red calico:
  4 - C

from dark red calico:
  4 - C

For Block 4 (Four Corners) cut the following:

from green solid:
  4 - E

from dark red calico:
  1 square 8½ × 8½ inches

from light green calico:
  4 strips, each 2½ × 8½ inches

For Block 5 (Shadow) cut the following:

from red solid:
  4 - C

from dark red calico:
  1 strip 1⁵⁄₁₆ × 30 inches

from red calico:
  1 strip 1⁵⁄₁₆ × 30 inches

from green calico:
  2 strips, each 1⁵⁄₁₆ × 30 inches

For Block 6 (Card Trick) cut the following:

from green solid:
  6 - B

from light green calico:
  4 - B

from dark green calico:
  6 - B

For Block 7 (Nine Patch) cut the following:

from green solid:
  1 - A

from red calico:
  4 - A

from dark red calico:
  4 - A

For Block 8 (Windmill) cut the following:

from green solid:
  1 strip 2½ × 26 inches

from dark green calico:
  1 strip 2½ × 26 inches

from light green calico:
  1 strip 2½ × 26 inches

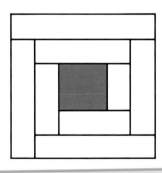

Block 1

Directions

To make Block 1: Log Cabin

Refer to the assembly diagram for Block 1.

1. With right sides facing, stitch light green calico strip (A) to the right edge of the red square.

2. Next, stitch dark green calico strip (B) to the bottom edge of the unit.

3. With right sides facing, stitch red calico strip (C) to the left side edge of the unit. Next, stitch red calico 2 strip (D) to the top edge of the unit.

4. Continue in this way with the remaining strips, (E), (F), (G), and (H) as shown in the assembly diagram. Press seams to one side.

To make Block 2: Basket

Refer to the assembly diagram for Block 2.

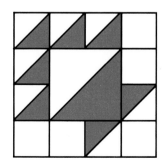

Block 2

121

1. With right sides facing, stitch all the dark green calico triangles to the light green calico triangles to make squares. Press seams to one side.

2. With right sides facing, stitch 3 pieced squares together, ending with a solid light green square to make a row of 4 squares. This is Row 1.

3. Next, stitch a pieced square to the top edge of another pieced square. Then stitch this unit to the left side edge of the large pieced square. Press seams to one side.

4. With right sides facing, stitch a plain square to the top edge of a pieced square. Stitch this unit to the right side of the large pieced square.

5. Join 2 plain green squares, followed by a pieced square, then another plain square, to make the bottom row.

6. With right sides facing, join all 3 rows. Press seams to one side.

To make Block 3: Pinwheel

Refer to the assembly diagram for Block 3.

1. With right sides facing, stitch the dark red calico triangles to the red calico triangles to make 4 squares. Press seams to one side.

2. With right sides facing, join 2 squares to make a row. Make 2 rows.

3. With right sides facing, join the rows. Press seams to one side.

To make Block 4: Four Corners

Refer to the assembly diagram for Block 4.

1. With right sides facing, join a light green calico strip to one side of the dark red calico square. Press seams to one side.

2. Next, stitch a green solid square to each short end of the remaining 2 strips.

3. With right sides facing, attach these strips to the top and bottom edges of the dark red calico square. Press seams to one side.

To make Block 5: Shadow

Refer to the assembly diagram for Block 5.

1. With right sides facing, stitch the 4 calico strips together as shown along the long edges. (See the directions for strip piecing on page 16.)

2. Use template C to mark and cut out 4 triangles from the joined strips.

3. With right sides facing, join each pieced triangle to a solid red triangle to make 4 squares.

4. With right sides facing, stitch 2 squares together to make a row. Repeat with the other 2 squares.

5. Next, stitch the 2 rows together along the long edge. Press seams to one side.

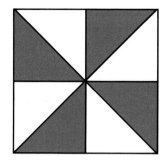

Block 3

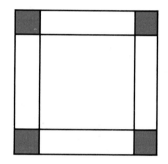

Block 4

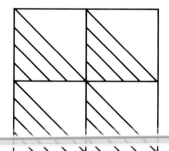

Block 5

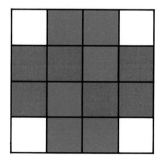

Block 6

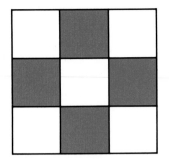

Block 7

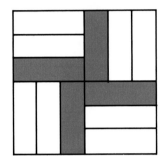

Block 8

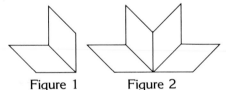

Figure 1   Figure 2

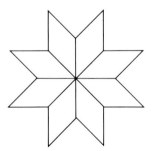

Figure 3

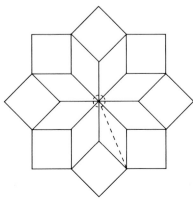

Figure 4

To make Block 6: Card Trick

Refer to the assembly diagram for Block 6 (see page 123).

1. With right sides facing, stitch 4 squares together as shown to make a row. Press seams. Make 4 rows in this way.

2. With right sides facing, join the 4 rows along the long edges. Press seams to one side.

To make Block 7: Nine Patch

Refer to the assembly diagram for Block 7.

1. With right sides facing, join 3 squares as shown to make a row. Press seams to one side. Make 3 rows in this way.

2. Next, with right sides facing, join all rows. Open seams and press.

To make Block 8: Windmill

Refer to the assembly diagram for Block 8.

1. With right sides facing, stitch all 3 strips together as shown along the long edges. (See the strip-piecing directions on page 16.) Press seams to one side.

2. Measure and cut the pieced fabric into 6½-inch segments.

3. With right sides facing, join 2 segments as shown to make a row. Make 2 rows in this way.

4. Next, join the rows. Press seams to one side.

To assemble tree skirt

1. With right sides facing, stitch 2 diamond pieces together along one edge, as shown in Figure 1. Make 4 sections in this way. Press seams to one side.

2. With right sides facing, stitch 2 of the sections together along one edge, as shown in Figure 2. Repeat with the remaining 2 sections to create 2 halves of the skirt.

3. With right sides facing, stitch the 2 halves together along the long edge, as shown in Figure 3.

4. See Figure 4. With right sides facing, stitch one side of a block to one raw edge of a diamond piece. When you get to the inside corner, leave the needle in the fabric. Lift the presser foot and turn the fabric so you can stitch down the adjoining side of the block. Replace the presser foot and stitch down that side.

5. Continue to join all 8 blocks in this way. Press seams to one side.

To finish

1. Refer to Figure 4, which shows a dotted line from point to point on one diamond piece. Cut the tree skirt open along this line on your fabric.

2. Using a plate or a compass, draw and cut a 6-inch circle in the center of the fabric (see dotted line on Figure 4).

3. Pin the seam binding to enclose the raw edge around the inner circle, down the slit, and around the entire edge of the tree skirt. Stitch all around.

COUNTRY TREE SKIRT TEMPLATES

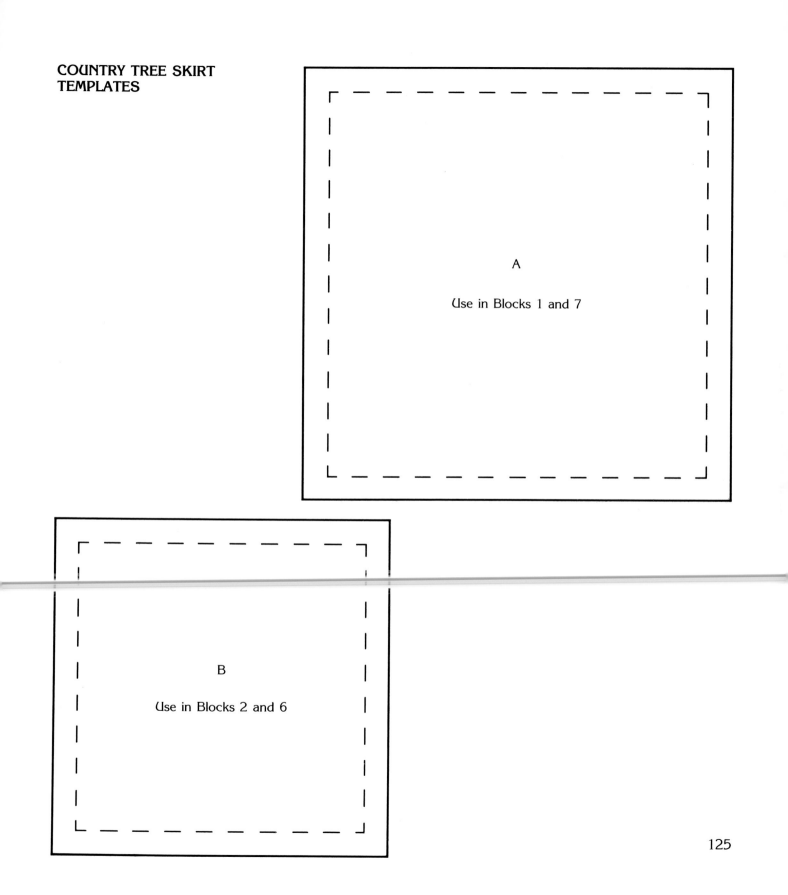

A

Use in Blocks 1 and 7

B

Use in Blocks 2 and 6

125

COUNTRY TREE SKIRT TEMPLATES

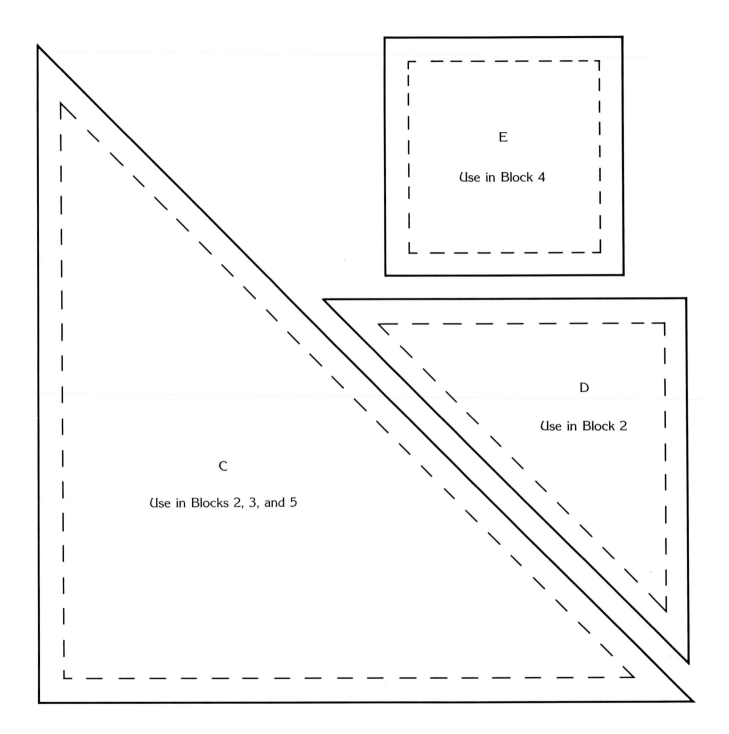

E

Use in Block 4

D

Use in Block 2

C

Use in Blocks 2, 3, and 5

COUNTRY TREE SKIRT DIAMOND PATTERN

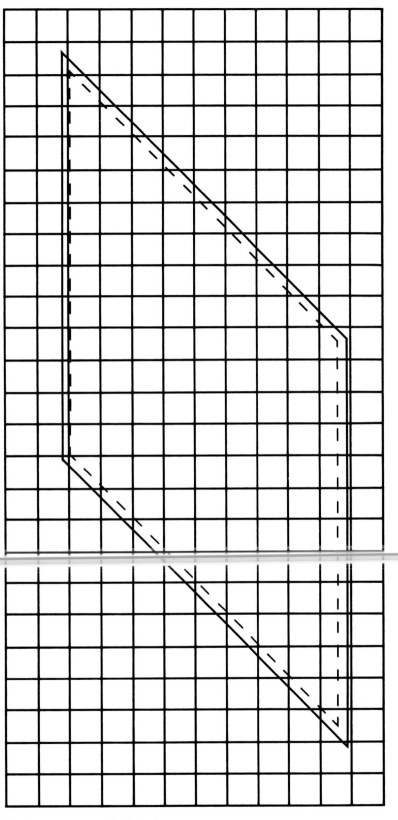

Each square equals 1 inch

127

Country Ornaments

These four patchwork ornaments are made from the scrap fabrics left over from the Country Tree Skirt on page 120. You can create a country theme by making enough ornaments to cover the entire tree. If you have plenty of scraps, this would be an economical as well as a delightful way to decorate for the holidays. Each ornament is 4 × 4 inches and could be filled with potpourri for sachets as well.

Materials (for 4 ornaments)

scraps of red and green solids
scraps of red calicos (light and darker shades)
scraps of green calicos (light and darker shades)
thin quilt batting (4 × 4 inches for each ornament)
½ yard ¼-inch green seam binding
½ yard ¼-inch red seam binding
½ yard green rickrack
1 yard gold twist thread for hanging
embroidery needle
tracing paper
cardboard

Cutting List

Note: All measurements include a ¼-inch seam allowance.

Trace patterns A, B, C, D, E, and F and transfer to cardboard for templates (see page 11).

For Ornament 1 (Pinwheel) cut the following:

from dark red calico:
  4 - A

from red calico:
  4 - A

For Ornament 2 (Nine Patch) cut the following:

from dark red calico:
  4 - B

from red calico:
  4 - C

from green solid:
  1 - C

For Ornament 3 (Four Corners) cut the following:

from dark green calico:
  1 - D

from green solid:
  4 - E

from light green calico:
  4 - F

For Ornament 4 (Windmill) cut the following:

from green solid:
    1 strip 1 × 8 inches

from green calico:
    1 strip 1 × 8 inches

from light green calico:
    1 strip 1 × 8 inches

For each ornament cut the following:

from any fabric:
    1 backing piece 4½ × 4½ inches

from quilt batting:
    1 piece 4 × 4 inches

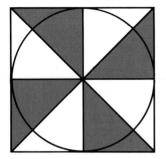

Ornament 1

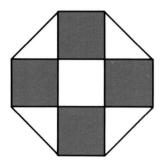

Ornament 2

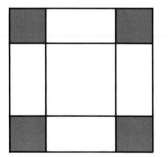

Ornament 3

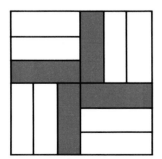

Ornament 4

Directions

To Make Ornaments

Ornament 1: Pinwheel

Refer to the assembly diagram for Ornament 1.

1. With right sides facing, join each dark red calico A piece to a red calico A piece to make squares. Press seams to one side.

2. Next, stitch 2 squares together as shown to make a row. Repeat with the remaining 2 squares.

3. With right sides facing, stitch the 2 rows together to make a block.

Ornament 2: Nine Patch

Refer to the assembly diagram for Ornament 2.

1. With right sides facing, stitch the short edge of a dark red calico B piece to each side of a red calico C piece to make a row. Make 2 rows in this way. One will be used for the top row and one for the bottom row.

2. Next, stitch a red calico C piece to each side of the green solid C piece to make the middle row. Press seams to one side.

3. With right sides facing, stitch all 3 rows together to make a block.

Ornament 3: Four Corners

Refer to the assembly diagram for Ornament 3.

1. With right sides facing, stitch a green solid E piece to each short end of a light green calico F piece to make the top row. Repeat for the bottom row.

2. Next, stitch the remaining F pieces to each side of the dark green calico D piece to make the middle row.

3. With right sides facing, stitch all 3 rows together to make a block. Press seams to one side.

Ornament 4: Windmill

Refer to the assembly diagram for Ornament 4.

1. With right sides facing, stitch all 3 strips together along the long edges as shown. (See the directions for strip piecing on page 16.)

2. Measure and cut the pieced fabric into 2-inch sections.

3. With right sides facing, stitch 2 sections together as shown to make a row. Repeat with the remaining 2 sections.

4. With right sides facing, stitch the 2 rows together as shown to make a block. Press seams to one side.

To finish

For all ornaments: Pin each pieced ornament top to a batting piece and then a backing piece.

Ornament 1: Pinwheel

1. Using a compass or round object, mark a 4½-inch circle on the pieced fabric. Cut through all 3 layers on the marked line.
2. Pin red seam binding over the raw edge around the ornament and stitch all around.

Ornament 2: Nine Patch

1. Trim the backing and the batting to the same shape as the ornament top.
2. Turn the raw edges of the backing and the top to the inside ¼ inch all around and press.
3. Pin the green rickrack binding to the ornament around the edge and stitch all around.

Ornament 3: Four Corners

1. Turn the raw edges of the backing and the top to the inside ¼ inch all around and press.
2. Slip-stitch all around.

Ornament 4: Windmill

1. Pin green seam binding so it encases the raw edges of the ornament.
2. Stitch all around.

To hang

1. Cut the gold twist thread into 8-inch lengths. Using an embroidery needle, thread a piece through the top edge or corner of each ornament.
2. Tie the ends in a knot and hang.

COUNTRY ORNAMENTS TEMPLATES

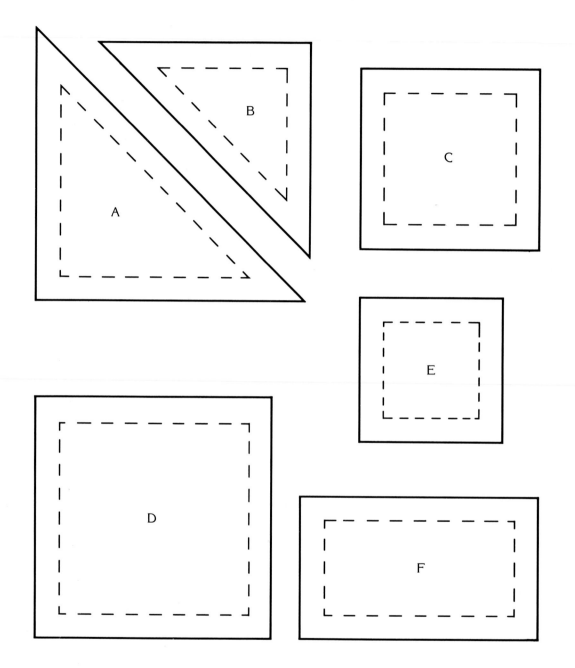

Christmas Star Quilt

While the Log Cabin is a traditional pattern, it can look completely different each time it's made depending on the quiltmaker and his or her choice of fabrics. The rich colors that Nancy Moore used to make this quilt are outstanding. We call it a Christmas quilt because it seems so right for the holidays. However, whenever you make this 37 × 37½-inch quilted throw or wall hanging, it will be right at home in any room.

Materials

Note: All yardages are figured for 45-inch-wide fabric.

    1¼ yards navy blue calico 1 (includes backing)
    1 yard cream calico
    ½ yard red solid
    ½ yard navy blue calico 2
    ½ yard navy blue print 3
    ⅛ yard red calico
    quilt batting 37 × 37 inches
    1 skein red embroidery floss
    embroidery needle
    tracing paper
    cardboard
    40-inch-long ¼-inch dowel for hanging (optional)

Cutting List

Note: All measurements include a ¼-inch seam allowance.

Trace patterns A, B, C, D, E, F, G, H, and I and transfer to cardboard for templates (see page 11). Trace around the templates on the wrong side of the fabrics as indicated on the next page.

133

Figure 1

Figure 2

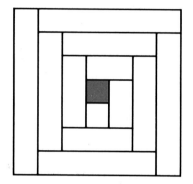

Figure 3

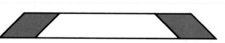

Figure 4

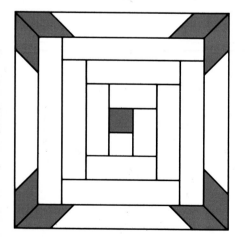

Figure 5

Cut the following:

from navy blue calico 1:
    1 backing piece 40 × 40 inches
    16 - D
    16 - E

from cream calico:
    16 - A
    16 - B
    16 - C
    16 - D
    16 - E
    16 - F
    32 - H

from red solid:
    16 - A
    128 - I

from navy blue calico 2:
    16 - F
    16 - G

from navy blue print 3:
    32 - H

from red calico:
    16 - B
    16 - C

Directions

To make a block

1. With right sides facing, stitch the bottom edge of a red solid A piece to the top edge of a cream calico A piece. Press seams to one side.

2. Next, with right sides facing, stitch the long edge of a cream calico B piece to the right side of this unit as shown in Figure 1. Press seams to one side.

3. With right sides facing, stitch the long edge of a red calico B piece to the top edge of the unit. Next, join a red calico C piece to the left side as shown in Figure 2. Press seams to the dark sides.

4. Refer to Figure 3 and continue by stitching a cream calico C piece to the bottom edge of the unit, a cream calico D piece to the right side, a navy blue calico 1 D piece to the top edge, and a navy blue calico 1 E piece to the left side. Press seams to the dark sides.

5. Repeat this sequence using a cream calico E piece on the bottom, then a cream calico F piece on the right, followed by a navy blue calico 2 F piece on the top, and then a navy blue calico 2 G piece on the left. Press seams to one side (see Figure 2).

6. Refer to Figure 4. With right sides facing, join a red solid I piece to each short, angled end of a cream calico H piece. Make 2. Stitch a red I piece to each angled end of a navy blue print 3 H piece in the same way. Make 2.

7. With right sides facing, stitch 1 of the cream/red strips to the bottom edge of the block as shown in Figure 5. Repeat along the right side edge. Next, stitch the blue/red strips to the top and left side edges of this unit. Press seams to one side.

8. With right sides facing, stitch the corner I pieces together from point to point to finish the block. Make 16 blocks in this way.

To join blocks

Refer to the assembly diagram.

1. Arrange the blocks into 4 rows of 4 blocks each as shown.

2. With right sides facing, stitch the first block to the second block along one side edge. Press seams to one side.

3. Continue to join all 4 blocks in this way to make a row. Make all 4 rows in this way.

To join rows

Refer to the assembly diagram.

1. With right sides facing, stitch the bottom edge of the first row to the top edge of the second row. Press seams to one side.

2. Continue to join all 4 rows in this way.

Christmas Star Quilt Assembly Diagram

To tie quilt

1. With wrong sides facing, pin the pieced top, batting, navy blue calico 1 and backing together.

2. Starting at the center and working to the outer edges in a starburst pattern, take long, loose basting stitches through all 3 layers (see page 14).

3. Tie the quilt with red embroidery floss at the center of each star in the following way: Insert the embroidery needle threaded with an 8-inch length of floss from the top through all layers and bring it back up as close to the first stitch as possible. Tie a knot and clip the ends of the floss to within ½ inch.

To finish

1. Trim the batting ½ inch smaller than the quilt top all around. Trim the backing piece so it's 1 inch larger than the quilt top on each side and bottom edge, and 2 inches larger at the top.

2. Turn the side and bottom raw edges of the backing to the inside ¼ inch and press. Then turn these edges over onto the quilt top to create ½-inch border.

3. Turn the top raw edge of the backing to the inside ½ inch and press. Turn this edge over onto the top of the quilt for a 1-inch border, which will also create a channel across the top. Slip-stitch to the quilt top.

4. Slip the dowel through the channel and hang. Or, hang by attaching strips of Velcro® to the back top and bottom edges of the quilt. Attach corresponding Velcro® strips to the wall.

CHRISTMAS STAR QUILT TEMPLATES

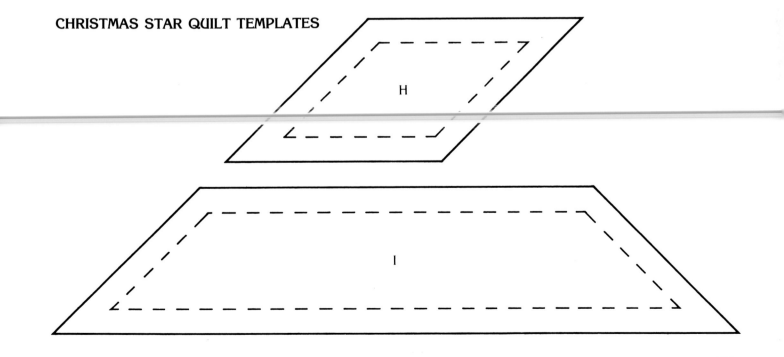

CHRISTMAS STAR QUILT TEMPLATES

Pine Tree Wall Hanging

Rows of staggered pine trees on a white quilted background create a handsome wall hanging. Each tree is created from the same template and scraps of different-colored calicos. For a bold green-and-white design, you could use only green prints for all the trees. The finished size is 24×26 inches.

Materials

Note: All yardages are figured for 45-inch-wide fabric.

1 yard white solid
1 yard green calico for backing
⅛ yard dark green calico for tree trunks
scraps of calicos for treetops
quilt batting 24×26 inches
tracing paper
cardboard
light pencil or fabric marker
Velcro® tabs for hanging

Cutting List

Note: All measurements include a ¼-inch seam allowance.

Trace patterns A, B, C, D, E, and F and transfer to cardboard for templates (see page 11).

Cut the following:

from white solid:

~~2 strips, each 2×23½ inches~~
    (side borders)
2 strips, each 2×20½ inches
    (top and bottom borders)
52 - B
26 - C
 8 - E
 4 - F

from green calico backing fabric:
    backing piece 25×27 inches

~~from dark green calico:~~
    13 - D

from calico scraps:
    26 - A (2 of the same fabric)

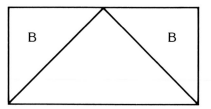

Figure 1

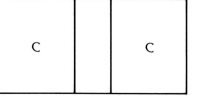

Figure 2

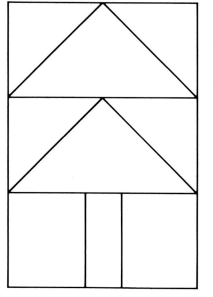

Figure 3

Directions

To make a block

1. Refer to Figure 1. With right sides facing, stitch the long edge of 1 white B piece to one short edge of an A piece. Press seams to one side.

2. Next, stitch another B piece to the other short edge of the A piece to make a rectangle, as shown in Figure 1. Press seams to one side.

3. Using the same-color A piece, repeat step 1.

4. Refer to Figure 2. With right sides facing, stitch the right side edge of a white C piece to the left long edge of a dark green calico D piece. Then, stitch the right side of the D piece to the left side of another white C piece. Press seams to one side.

5. With right sides facing, stitch all 3 sections together to make a tree block as shown in Figure 3.

6. Press seams to one side. Make 13 tree blocks in this way.

To join blocks

Refer to the assembly diagram. Blocks are joined in vertical rows.

1. With right sides facing, stitch the bottom edge of a tree block to the top edge of a white E piece. Next, stitch the bottom edge of the white E piece to the top edge of another tree block.

2. Continue with another white E piece and then another tree block in the same way to complete vertical Row 1. Press seams to one side. Make 3 rows in this way; they will be Rows 1, 3, and 5.

3. With right sides facing, stitch the bottom edge of a white F piece to the top edge of a tree block.

4. Next, stitch the bottom edge of the tree block to the top edge of a white E piece.

5. Continue with another tree block and then another white F piece to complete vertical Row 2. Press seams to one side. Make 2 rows in this way; they will be Rows 2 and 4.

To join rows

1. With right sides facing and seams aligned, stitch the right side edge of Row 1 to the left side edge of vertical Row 2. Press seams to one side.

2. Continue with Row 3. Join all 5 rows in this way to make the quilt top. Press seams to one side.

To add borders

1. With right sides facing, join one $2 \times 2\frac{1}{2}$-inch white border strip to the top edge of the quilt top.

2. Next, join the other $2 \times 20\frac{1}{2}$-inch white border strip to the bottom edge of the quilt top. Press all seams.

3. With right sides facing, stitch the two $2 \times 25\frac{1}{2}$-inch white border strips to the sides of the quilt top in the same way. Press seams.

140

To quilt

1. Refer to the assembly diagram and position the A template on the fabric as shown. Using a ruler and a light pencil or a fabric marker, mark around the template to draw the tree shapes on the white background between the calico trees.

2. Cut the backing piece 1 inch larger than the quilt top all around.

3. With wrong sides facing, pin the quilt top, batting, and backing together.

4. Baste through all 3 layers with long, loose stitches in a starburst pattern.

5. Using small running stitches, quilt along the premarked lines and ⅛ inch on the outside of all seam lines of each calico tree.

To finish

1. When all quilting has been completed, remove basting stitches.

2. Trim the batting ½ inch smaller than the quilt top all around.

3. Turn the raw edges of the backing to the inside ¼ inch on each side and press. Next, fold the backing forward over the top edge of the quilt to create a ½-inch green border all around. Blindstitch to the quilt top.

4. Attach a Velcro® tab to the back of each corner and in the center of each side. Attach corresponding tabs to the wall where it will hang.

Pine Tree Wall Hanging
Assembly Diagram

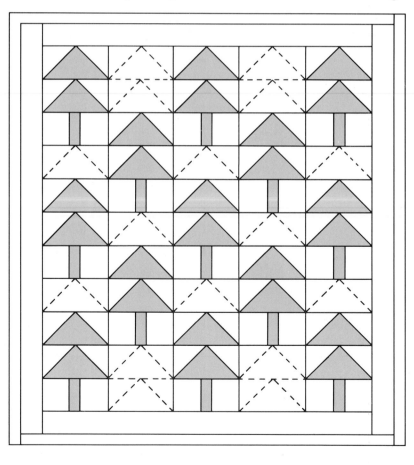

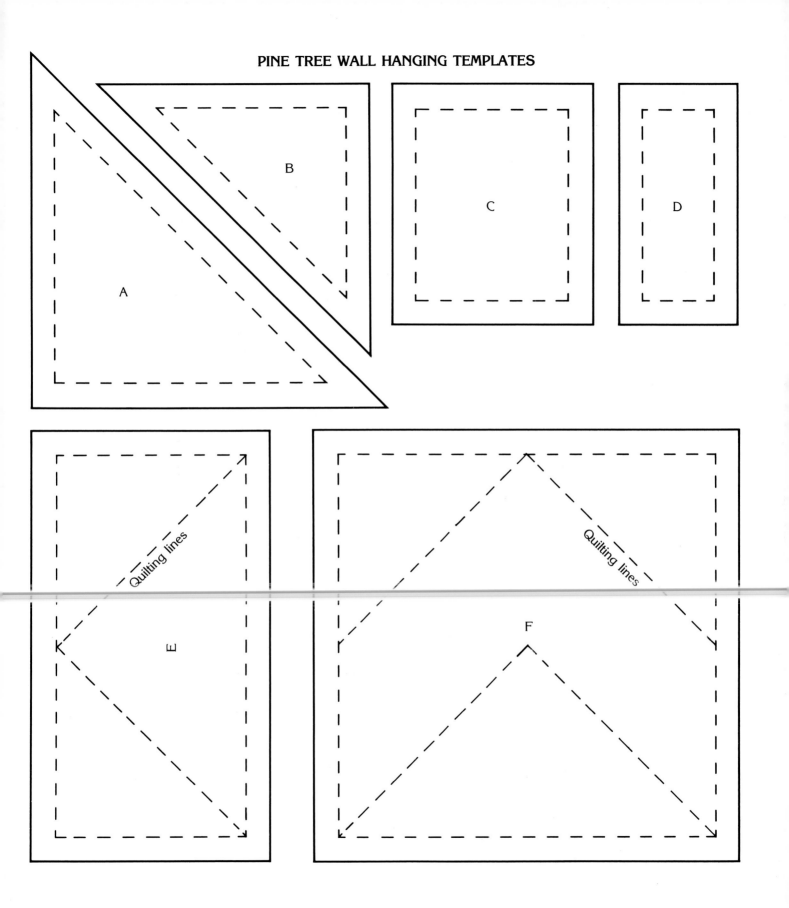

PINE TREE WALL HANGING TEMPLATES

A

B

C

D

E

Quilting lines

F

Quilting lines

Index

All of us at Meredith® Press are dedicated to offering you, our customer, the best books we can create. We are particularly concerned that all of the instructions for making projects are clear and accurate. Please address your correspondence to: Customer Service Department, Meredith® Press, Meredith Corporation, 150 East 52nd Street, New York, NY 10022.

Small Patchwork & Quilting is the sixth in a series of quilting books. If you would like the first five books in the series, please write to: Better Homes and Gardens Books, P.O. Box 10670, Des Moines, IA 50309-3400, or call 1-800-678-2665.

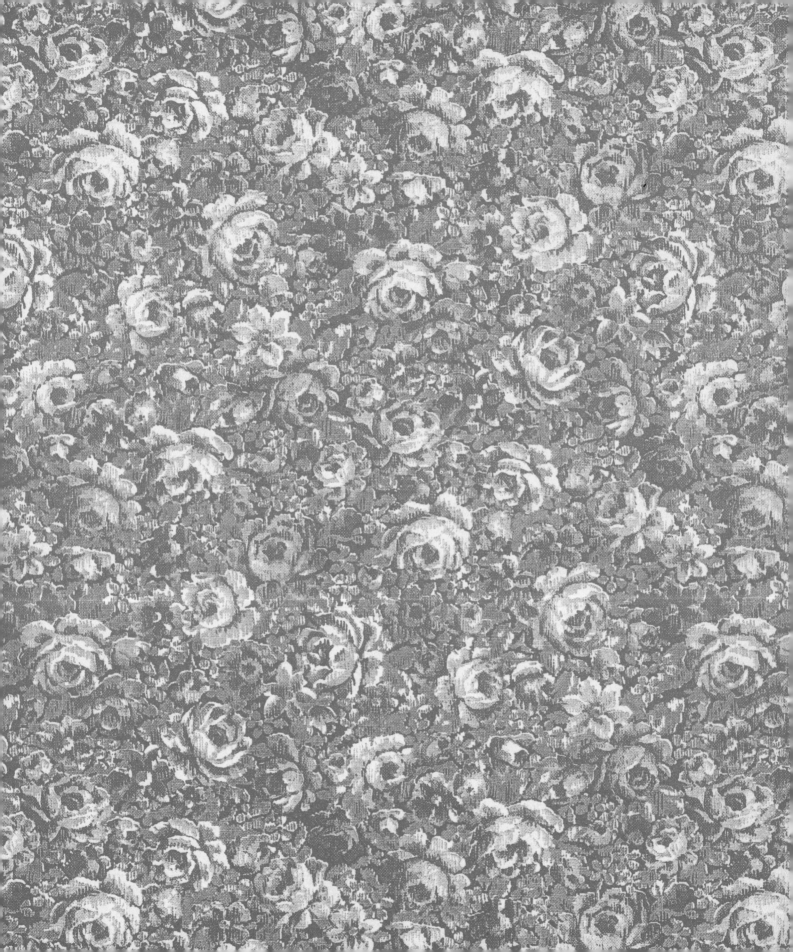